Investing in
Emerging Markets

The Rules of the Game

_____

William B. Gamble

Apress®

Investing in Emerging Markets: The Rules of the Game

Copyright © 2011 by William Gamble

ISBN-13 (pbk): 978-1-4302-3825-6

ISBN-13 (electronic): 978-1-4302-3826-3

Trademarked names may appear in this book. Rather than use a trademark symbol with every occurrence of a trademarked name, we use the names only in an editorial fashion and to the benefit of the trademark owner, with no intention of infringement of the trademark.

President and Publisher: Paul Manning
Lead Editor: Jeff Olson
Editorial Board: Steve Anglin, Mark Beckner, Ewan Buckingham, Gary Cornell, Morgan Ertel, Jonathan Gennick, Jonathan Hassell, Robert Hutchinson, Michelle Lowman, James Markham, Matthew Moodie, Jeff Olson, Jeffrey Pepper, Douglas Pundick, Ben Renow-Clarke, Dominic Shakeshaft, Gwenan Spearing, Matt Wade, Tom Welsh
Coordinating Editor: Adam Heath
Copy Editor: Chandra Clarke
Compositor: Mary Sudul
Indexer: SPi Global
Cover Designer: Anna Ishchenko

Distributed to the book trade worldwide by Springer Science+Business Media, LLC., 233 Spring Street, 6th Floor, New York, NY 10013. Phone 1-800-SPRINGER, fax (201) 348-4505, e-mail orders-ny@springer-sbm.com, or visit www.springeronline.com.

For information on translations, please e-mail rights@apress.com, or visit www.apress.com.

Apress and friends of ED books may be purchased in bulk for academic, corporate, or promotional use. eBook versions and licenses are also available for most titles. For more information, reference our Special Bulk Sales–eBook Licensing web page at www.apress.com/bulk-sales.

For Louise

Contents

About the Author

William B. Gamble, JD, LLM, Ex MBA, KSC, is an international lawyer and consultant specializing in emerging markets. His weekly columns are published in the financial newspapers *Alrroya* in Dubai, and *MoneyLife* in Mumbai. His letters have been published in the *Wall Street Journal* and 28 of them in the *Financial Times*. He has published articles in *Foreign Affairs* and *Harvard International Review*. He has been quoted in MarketWatch, *The New York Times, USA TODAY, The Far Eastern Economic Review, The Asset, The International Herald Tribune, The South China Morning Post, Sankei Shimbun*, and *The Investment Professional*. He has appeared on ABC, CNN Asia, Bloomberg, Fox, CNBC, NPR, NDTV Profit (India) and other television and radio stations around the world. His other books are *Investing in China* (2002) and *Freedom: America's Competitive Advantage in the Global Market* (2007). As a retained speaker for the CFA, he has lectured to societies in 12 countries and 11 US cities as well as other conferences all over the world.

Emerging Markets vs. Marketing Emerging Markets

Chenggong is shiny new town in China that seems to represent the epitome of the Chinese miracle. For years, Western media, economists, financial analysts, brokerage firms, pundits, government officials—and certainly the Chinese themselves—have perpetuated the concept of unlimited growth.

And it is not just China. Thanks to the economist Jim O'Neill and the marketing machine at Goldman Sachs, the idea of limitless growth has been extended, through the acronym BRIC, to Brazil, Russia, India, as well as China. Now it is not only the BRIC countries that have Wall Street's attention. Vast fortunes can also be made by buying into virtually any emerging market and waiting. The truth of the emerging market story seems plain to any Western traveler who has seen cities sprout from rice paddies all over Asia—cities exactly like Chenggong.

In 2003, Chenggong did not exist. Now the many high-rise apartment houses stand resplendent next to wide, tree-lined streets. Thirteen marble-clad buildings are for the local government, which is famous the world over for getting things done, done right, and done on time. Nor is education neglected in Chenggong. There are large campuses for the region's universities, ready to turn out the next generation of tech-savvy engineers. To feed these places of higher learning, a new high school has been built with all the latest facilities. Even the climate seems to help.

Chenggong is only 12 miles (20 kilometers) from Kunming, the provincial capital. It's almost a suburb. Located in the province of Yunnan, these cities enjoy short, cool, dry winters with mild days and crisp nights. In the summer it does get humid, but not anywhere near the level of other subtropical cities. Chenggong has a low latitude and a high elevation, guaranteeing temperatures that rarely dip below freezing in the winter and do not go above 85 degrees Fahrenheit (30°C) in the summer.

The climate is not the only beneficial aspect of Chenggong's location. Kunming has been a center of trade since the eighth century. In ancient times, caravans from central China travelled through Kunming on their way to Southeast Asia. This trade has not only continued, but expanded, thanks to ambitious building projects. The road from Kunming to Bangkok has just been completed, as has the road joining the city to Vietnam. Soon, these projects will be followed by links to Myanmar (Burma). While high-speed rail in the United States flounders amid regulations and political bickering, a new high-speed rail system is being built to connect Kunming to Shanghai, 2000 kilometers away. The 20 kilometers between Chenggong and Kunming will soon be connected, thanks to a 163-kilometer light rail network.

In a very poor country that a generation ago was mired in poverty, in a region far from the burgeoning coast, Chenggong seems to be a shining example to the world of the success of the Chinese system in particular and the promise of profit in emerging markets.

But there is one small problem.

Chenggong is empty. No one lives there.

As Chenggong Goes, So Goes China

But it is not just Chenggong. There are empty buildings all over China. Jack Rodman is the president of Distressed Solutions LLC. According to a recent news article, "he keeps a slide show on his computer of empty office buildings in Beijing, his home since 2002. The tally: 55, with another dozen candidates."[1] According to Rodman, the vacancy rate in Beijing is over 50%. But that was in 2010. The real estate building craze in China has been going on for years.

---

[1] "Beijing Seen Vacant for 50% as Chanos Predicts Crash (Update1)," *Bloomberg*, www.bloomberg.com/apps/news?pid=newsarchive&sid=a6i2PSZD.Jr4, February 12, 2010.

Two years ago during a trip to the city of Guiyang, the capital of Guizhou Province—which is next to the province of Yunnan and so not far from Chenggong—fund manager Stephan van der Mersch made a startling discovery. "I thought I'd seen insane excess in the past—200 thousand-square-meter malls completely empty next to apartment complexes with 40,000 units and 30% occupancy rates, etc. etc. But what we saw over there is rather hard to fathom."[2] What he saw was "well over a hundred twenty-plus story buildings" spread over 11.6 square miles (30 square kilometers) of farmland well north of Guiyang. Every building was either incomplete, under construction, or empty. Van der Mersch guesstimated that he was looking at about $10 billion worth of bad loans.[3]

Videos of China's empty real estate have been multiplying on the Internet. One such video[4] is about the New South China Mall, which was begun in 2005. When it was built, it was the largest mall in the world. Most of its stores have never been occupied by a single tenant. The present owner, Beijing University, purchased it from the developers, who went bust. The university hired international consultants to make it work. The consultants failed and blamed the location.

But is the location that bad? Halfway between Hong Kong and Guangzhou, the mall sits in the middle of the famous workshop of the world. In this industrialized corridor, most of the world's appliances, from televisions to air conditioners, are manufactured. Yet in the birthplace of China's economic boom, the mall sits empty. To make matters worse, the owners continue to build. They feel that if they expand another 200,000 square meters to over a million, they can make money.

Yet despite the vacancies, real estate prices keep rising. Back in Chenggong, a local real estate agent, Mr. Xin, has purchased eight apartments, hoping to make a killing: "I think it is a good idea to invest now before the property prices in Chenggong start to rocket."[5] Perhaps he is right.

Most of the world's investors seem to think so, and there is plenty of evidence: "According to Standard Chartered, the average land price in China

[2] Michael Pettis, "China: A Look at the Real Estate Picture," seekingalpha.com/article/149849-china-a-look-at-the-real-estate-picture, July 20, 2009.

[3] Ibid.

[4] "Dongguan Ghost Mall Haunts China's Property Boom: Video," *Bloomberg*, www.bloomberg.com/news/2011-01-12/dongguan-ghost-mall-haunts-china-s-property-boom-video.html, January 11, 2011.

[5] Geoff Dyer, "China: No one home," *Financial Times*, www.ft.com, February 21, 2010.

increased by 106% last year [2009]. That includes an increase of more than 200% in Shanghai, nearly 400% in Guangzhou, and 876% in Wenzhou." The market cooled slightly in 2010, but not much. Despite government efforts, land prices still rose over 70%.

Chenggong an Emblem of Success. Really?

Many economists and financial experts think that the boom in real estate is just more evidence of the success of the Chinese model. The extraordinary building spree might have a few kinks in it but, given China's remarkable growth rates, cities like Chenggong will fill up fast enough. Kunming is already overcrowded and choked with traffic. As soon as the transportation links are established, the surplus buildings in Chenggong will fill up. As soon as more extensive rail and road networks are put in place, Chinese trade with Southeast Asia will double, along with the demand for better housing.

This growth is not limited to China. The materials used to build Chenggong have come from all over the world. The Chinese boom has meant a boom in commodities that has benefitted everyone from Australian iron ore miners to Brazilian soybean farmers. The result has been rapid growth in most emerging markets, which are ever more dependent on Chinese demand.

This growth has led many investors and pundits to wax eloquently about a shift in the world's global axis. One of Europe's most renowned stock-pickers, Anthony Bolton, is so bullish on China that he has put off retirement, relocating to Hong Kong to launch a China-focused mutual fund. According to Mr. Bolton, "The centre of gravity is clearly shifting to this part of the world and I want to play a part in it while I can. The investment opportunity is simply too great to pass up."[6]

Commentators with Open Eyes

In contrast stands Jim Chanos, a successful hedge fund manager who won his spurs and his fortune by identifying and shorting seriously overvalued assets, most famously Enron. His view of China is quite blunt: "They're on a 'treadmill to hell,' and they can't get off it."[7] Another hedge fund manager,

---

[6] Sundeep Tucker, Jamil Anderlini, and Robert Cookson, "A reputation at risk in China," *Financial Times*, January 4, 2010.

[7] Jim Chanos, The Charlie Rose Show, www.charlierose.com/download/transcript/10960, April 12, 2010.

Hugh Hendry, went Chanos one better. He went to Guangzhou's gleaming new towers with his video camera and filmed the empty buildings, putting the videos up on YouTube where they can be seen to this day.[8] Hendry's and Chanos's point is that these buildings, like the ones in Chenggong, are empty, and so either are or will become nonperforming loans on the books of Chinese banks.[9] In short, the Chinese have a massive real estate bubble like the subprime crash in the US. They do have a point.

Professor Victor Shih of Northwestern University "estimates that local governments have amassed about 11.4 trillion yuan (around $1.7 trillion) worth of debt at the end of 2009, or roughly a third of China's gross domestic product for that year, and that they're likely to borrow a further 12.7 trillion yuan by the end of 2011."[10] The bad news is that Professor Shih thinks that 25% of these debts will go bad.

According to Li Daokui, a professor at the top-ranked Tsinghua University and a member of the Chinese central bank's monetary policy committee, "the housing market problem in China is actually much, much more fundamental, much bigger than the housing market problem in the US and UK before your financial crisis. It is more than [just] a bubble problem."[11]

So the investor has a problem. You have some of the most prominent money managers and economists in the world with a fundamental disagreement over the second-largest economy in the world. They have wildly divergent opinions. How can the investor make sense of their very different advice?

One question investors have to ask is, if things are that bad, why hasn't the economy of China blown up? Why not a meltdown?

The answer is simple, and it will be the focus of this book. What is happening is that the rules in China—and the other countries profiled here—are different. When the rules change, so does the game.

---

[8] http://www.youtube.com/watch?v=ektMQGbW3wk.

[9] As of October 2011, Anthony Bolton's fund had lost all its profits, and Mr. Bolton decided to step down in 2013. Funds run by Chanos and Henry have soared.

[10] Dinny McMahon, "Victor Shih Sees Bank Bailout Redux," *Wall Street Journal*, http://blogs.wsj.com/chinarealtime/2010/03/17/victor-shih-sees-bank-bailout-redux/?KEYWORDS=Victor+Shih, March 17, 2010.

[11] Geoff Dyer, "China told property risk is worse than in US," *Financial Times*, www.ft.com, May 31, 2010.

Wall Street's Track Record

Emerging markets have recently enjoyed quite a run on Wall Street. Open any financial magazine or newspaper, or watch a financial news channel, and no doubt you will see a slick advertisement by some sort of fund manager or bank. The advertisement will undoubtedly feature an ethnically Asian person or someone in traditional Arabic dress. Behind the characters will be the shining towers of Shanghai (on one of its rare clear days) or Dubai. Airplanes, airports, and high-speed trains are always popular, as are bits of fancy telecommunications devices and impossibly well-tailored clothes. The copy will tell you all about the institution's global reach and how it understands everything about how to make money in the global market.

To start with, most of these companies do not know how to make money in any market. Each and every money manager, economist, and financial analyst has an impossible task. They are all trying to do one thing. They are trying to predict the future. They will fail. Their task is not made any easier by another problem, which I will discuss later in fuller detail. The information that they crunch in their massive and expensive hardware is simply wrong, and it is getting worse. The results are clear from their records in both developed and emerging markets.

In a recent conference held at King's College, Cambridge, a group of economists—including five Nobel laureates—could neither agree on the cause of the recent financial crisis in the developed Western countries nor the necessary remedies. They did agree "that the financial and economic crisis had exposed fatal flaws in their subject and ideas were urgently needed to keep economics relevant."[12] In a lecture last year, economics Nobel laureate and columnist Paul Krugman stated that most macroeconomics of the past 30 years was "spectacularly useless at best, and positively harmful at worst."[13] Ouch!

Money managers are some of the highest-paid professionals in the world. In theory, according to Professor Lynda Gratton of the London Business School, these giants of finance are paid huge sums because "they are particularly skillful, and . . . they have information that is valuable. Now, the interesting thing

---

[12] Chris Giles, "Economists clash on cause of crisis," *Financial Times*, www.ft.com, April 10, 2010.

[13] "The other-worldly philosophers," *The Economist*, www.economist.com/node/14030288?story_id=E1_TQDPDNRR, Jul 16, 2009.

from an academic perspective is that there isn't really any research to show that what they do is particularly skillful."[14]

But What About Hedge Funds?

Let us start with the stars of money managers: the people who run hedge funds and private equity firms. These financial geniuses and dealmakers are paid literally billions to invest other people's money, but do they actually make money?

Hedge funds did make a lot of money when they were new. According to Chicago-based data provider Hedge Fund Research, between 1990 and 2000 hedge funds were able to achieve an astonishing annual return of 18.74%.[15] They did this by exploiting opportunities in markets. Of course the great thing about competitive markets is that success breeds competition, subsequently driving down prices. In the more recent past, between 2000 and 2007, hedge fund returns have been far more modest—just an average annual return of 8.61%.[16]

Normally an 8.61% return would be considered ample, but not with hedge funds. These celebrity hedge fund managers command large fees. The old standard in the industry, 2 and 20 (2% of assets and 20% of profits), required hefty returns just to break even. A return of 8.61% would be reduced by 3.7% in fees. So the real return would be less than 5%, a return that is often available on investments with little or no risk.

But there can be more fees. Hedge fund managers' methods and strategies are often arcane and filled with all the mystery that the name "black box" implies. How can investors choose between them? Enter the Fund of Funds (FOFs), which turns hedge funds into something more like a mutual fund. To be safe, we are supposed to diversify our hedge fund bets in many different funds chosen by another group of highly paid money managers.

What do investors get for these extra charges? Not much. So far in 2011, regular hedge funds are down about 2%, and that does not include the 2% management fee. FOFs did even worse—they're off more than 6%! It is not surprising that FOFs' share of hedge funds assets under management has

---

[14] Stefan Stern, "Lunch with the FT: Lynda Gratton," *Financial Times*, www.ft.com, February 5, 2010.

[15] Sam Jones, "Hedge funds hope 'Volcker rule' will clip banks' wings," *Financial Times*, www.ft.com, June 30 2010.

[16] Ibid.

fallen from 43% to 34%.[17] Worse, one of the justifications for FOFs managers is that they have access to the best hedge funds. This might be a selling point, except that one of the exclusive hedge funds that these managers chose was run by Bernard Madoff.

The issue of Madoff is important for another reason: transparency. According to a study by New York University's Stern School of Business, one in five hedge fund managers misrepresents his or her fund or its performance to investors.[18]

What about private equity? What do investors get for extra fees and the risk of tying up their money for possibly years? Very little. According to a recently published survey, only half of the investors in private equity deals are seeing returns above 10%. Two years ago, only a fifth had such small returns. The number of successful investors with returns greater than 15% has fallen from 40% to 20%.[19] Perhaps the biggest indictment of private equity has to do with the firm Kohlberg Kravis Roberts (KKR).

KKR is a legendary private equity firm. The subject of both books and a film, it has been around since 1976. The firm is now going public. According to filings in 2007, the firm estimated its worth to be over $25 billion. It is now estimated to be worth only $6.4 billion, a decline of 76%. The shares of the founders, Henry Kravis and George Roberts, have declined from $6 billion each to $800 million.[20]

It is understandable that risky hedge funds and private equity firms might have variable returns, but what about the plain old run-of-the-mill mutual funds? Surely these are conservatively managed with consistent returns? Well, no.

In the past two decades, actively managed mutual funds in the aggregate have failed to beat the indexes. Investing in index funds, like Exchange-Traded Funds (ETFs), has proven to be more profitable than investing in a fund managed by an experienced, intelligent individual. Over the past 30 years, fund managers have been underexposed in bull markets and overexposed in bear

---

[17] Lex, "Funds of hedge funds," *Financial Times*, www.ft.com, June 23, 2010.

[18] Sam Jones, "One in five hedge fund managers found to be misrepresenting facts," *Financial Times*, www.ft.com, October 14, 2009.

[19] Martin Arnold, "Crisis takes toll on private equity returns," *Financial Times*, www.ft.com, June 13, 2010.

[20] Justin Baer, "KKR founders sitting on $800m stakes," *Financial Times*, www.ft.com, July 6, 2010.

markets.[21] Basically, they always end up chasing the markets and following the herd.

One would think that a human might be able to beat the averages, but that is really the problem. Managers don't beat the averages, because they are human. They fall prey to instincts and cognitive biases. In fact, one of the most successful managers essentially did nothing at all. For the past 20 years he parked 80% of his money in money market funds.[22]

Sophisticated . . . Guesses

The reality is that the financial industry does not have the skillset to actually make money. The reason is quite simple. Decisions made by financial professionals whether to buy or sell a particular asset are based on estimations, approximations, forecasts, projections, and predictions. These are often based upon the latest economic theories, historical averages, complex mathematical models, technical analysis, and even astrology. Regardless of what they are based on, they are still nothing more than guesses.

Worse, the financial industry's entire incentive system is designed to encourage short-term outlooks and trend following. Any asset class that has been performing strongly over the previous 12 months will attract 8 times more money than other sectors. Over the succeeding 12 months, the most popular sector lagged the average by 3%. "[I]nvestors were more Nostradumbus than Nostradamus. The average fund flow into what turned out to be the worst-performing sector over the subsequent 12-month period was $166 million; the average flow into the best was only $72 million."[23] Money managers' compensation is judged quarterly. If their metrics do not match the quarterly averages, they rapidly adjust, in a process called "window dressing," by selling stocks with large losses and purchasing Wall Street's most recent darlings near the end of the quarter.

It is not just the money managers that mislead investors. Rating agencies do as well. Take the famous Morningstar ratings. If you buy a five-star rated fund, you are safe, right? Millions of investors think so. During the carnage

[21] John Authers, "Active managers need to show their worth," *Financial Times*, www.ft.com, July 2, 2010.

[22] Mark Hulbert, "The tortoise vs. the hares," *MarketWatch*, www.marketwatch.com/story/top-adviser-since-1980-mostly-in-cash-2010-06-29, June 29, 2010.

[23] Buttonwood, "Investors tend to chase the latest fad," *The Economist*, www.economist.com/node/18529721, April 7, 2011.

of 2008, investors fled in droves to the perceived safety of better-rated funds. Three-star funds lost $111 billion in assets, four-star funds lost $14 billion, but five-star funds enjoyed $67.5 billion of net inflows. But Morningstar ratings are backward-looking, based on a fund's *past* performance. A recent study over the past ten years looked at the performance of 248 equity funds. At the beginning of the period, all the funds had five-star ratings. At the end of the period, just four still kept that rank. Almost 90% of the five-star US equity funds lagged their category averages both for other mutual funds and for their benchmarks.

Rating agencies like Moody's and S&P were trusted absolutely for their opinions on a variety of debt instruments. Before the 2008 meltdown the rating agencies gave top triple-A ratings on hundreds of billions of securities backed by risky US mortgages, which proved to be inaccurate. Many triple-A bonds were downgraded and proved in fact to be worthless. The rating agencies are now being sued for fraud and gross negligence. Their defense: they really are only issuing an opinion, which is their right under the free speech clause in the US constitution. Moreover, investors assume the risk of relying on their expertise. Quite an about-face after years of claiming almost divine status in judging the financial quality of a variety of securities!

Investors also listen to and read a variety of pundits with bated breath, waiting for a few pearls of wisdom as to where to invest. Some pundits, like Jim Cramer in the US, have achieved celebrity status. Yet these learned people are unable to make even vaguely accurate predictions. Professor Philip Tetlock from the University of California did a study of 82,361 forecasts by 284 people who made their living making forecasts. What he found was that "human beings who spend their lives studying the state of the world . . . are poorer forecasters than dart-throwing monkeys."[24]

Beware the "Story"

This is not to say that the dart-throwing monkeys can't do something right. Pundits and investment advisors are very, very good at marketing. Their favorite marketing tool is the "story" investment. These investments all have a credible story that seems to make enormous sense. Two rather infamous stories were the dot-com bubble and the housing bubble. In retrospect, the logic seems absurd, but at the time there were few people who did not get on board. Who wouldn't?

---

[24] Louis Menand, "Everybody's An Expert: Putting predictions to the test," *The New Yorker*, December 5, 2005.

The dot-com boom seemed to be the way to cash in on a wonderful new technology. The Internet has certainly changed many things. Despite Tom Friedman's assertions in *The World Is Flat*, the Internet and other technologies were not solely responsible for globalization. Such prosaic inventions like the shipping container and the passenger jet were probably more important. And no one even mentions the most important aspect of all. The General Agreement on Tariffs and Trade (GATT), the forerunner of the World Trade Organization, was crucial because it changed the rules. That is not to say that the Internet has not changed many things, but it was not, as Wall Street advertised, an ever-growing cash machine.

Neither was the housing market, although the story was just as compelling. As Will Rogers pointed out, land is a good investment because they are not making any more land. Housing prices had generally increased since the Great Depression. The rapid growth in real estate prices seemed so inevitable that no one ever considered that they could collapse; but collapse they did.

Myth of Constant Growth

Now it is the turn of emerging markets. These markets have been touted as another can't-lose investment. At the heart of the story are the BRIC markets. The acronym was coined by Goldman Sachs's economist Jim O'Neill in a 2001 paper entitled "Building Better Global Economic BRICs."

The thesis, like all good finance stories, was beguilingly simple. Four countries, Brazil, Russia, India, and China, encompass over 25% of the world's land coverage, and they hold 40% of the world's population. Since they make up a good portion of the world, it was just a matter of time before they became the four most dominant economies. What could be more obvious?

Besides, not only did these countries have huge land masses and large populations, their populations were relatively young. China was—and is—the BRIC poster child.

China has enjoyed spectacular growth over the last decade. For two decades China has had an astonishing average growth rate of over 9%. It has changed from a poor, backward, repressed, rural, Communist country isolated from the world to a middle-income country that is the workshop of the world and a center of world trade.

According to the hype, China is filled with one billion unstoppable capitalist entrepreneurs eager to make their mark on the global economy. The government, although nominally Communist, is filled with clever technocrats skillfully guiding this developing powerhouse from poverty to prosperity. What could go wrong? A real estate bubble, perhaps?

The China story is so seductive that it has rubbed off on the other BRICs. After the fall of the "License Raj"—a tradition of red tape and over-regulation—in 1992, India has enjoyed consistent growth as well. India has not been growing as fast or as long as China, but over the past six years it has enjoyed growth rates exceeding 8%.

By contrast, Russia and Brazil were far more developed than either India or China. Still, they seem to have made major strides. Russia threw off the yoke of Communism and the chaos of the immediate post-Communist era to become a major energy exporter. Brazil has been crippled by political instability and hyperinflation, and it was never able to achieve its promise until the success of the Real Plan under the finance minster and later president, Fernando Cardoso.

It is not just the ten years of excellent growth. It is also the contrast of vibrant BRICs and the turpitude of more mature markets. The crash of 2008 crippled most developed countries. Both the US and Europe are limping along with only slight growth. Japan has been trapped in a deflationary spiral for over 20 years. While China's economy was booming, Japan could barely eke out any positive growth at all until 2011, when China surpassed it as the world's second-largest economy.

According to the default swap market, emerging markets are also less risky than developed markets. The precise number is expressed as the percentage cost of insuring a country's debt against default within five years. The default risk for Spain is 2.56%. For Italy the risk is 1.82%. In contrast, the default risk for Mexico, Brazil, Chile, Russia, and even Indonesia is only 1.39%. China's risk was the same as the UK at .6%, but has been rising. It is now the same level as France.

It is not just sovereign debt that has been a reasonably intelligent investment. Many of the equity returns have been nothing less than breathtaking. Since 2001, the Korean market has increased 355%, Brazil's market 436%, Chile's market 439%, and India's market 470%. But these increases pale in comparison to Indonesia, with an increase of almost 900%, and Russia, with an increase of almost fourteen fold!

So are Wall Street and the rest of the pundits absolutely correct as usual? The developed markets are aging and their best years are behind them. The emerging markets are filled with youthful, unstoppable vigor. The economic center of gravity has permanently shifted and all you have to do is invest in these markets and wait ten years. Much better than even gold!

Nice idea and a great pitch. It has worked so well that there are now BRIC ETFs. The BRIC concept has entered the realm of foreign policy as China holds a conference of the BRIC countries. Jim O'Neil has pronounced South Africa ready to join as BRIC becomes BRICSA. There is now a rush for so-called frontier markets, which are markets like the BRICs were ten years ago, just aching for massive returns.

But there is another story—a far more important one. Economists and financial analysts are very fond of history. During the 2008 crash, there were endless stories comparing the 2008 crash with the 1929 crash that started the Great Depression. When looking at emerging markets, it would be wise to use a longer lens.

An Historical View of "Constant Growth"

Prior to 1992, India seemed to be stuck with the "Hindu" growth rate (3.5%). During the 1990s it was constantly being compared unfavorably with China, usually because commentators felt that there was something wrong with democracy. One reason for the Russian stock market's spectacular climb was its starting point. Russia defaulted on many of its debts in 1998. Both Korea and Indonesia were swept up in the Asian crises in 1997 when their economies and currencies collapsed. Like Greece, Ireland, and Portugal today, they had to accept bailouts. Peru's economy and stock market are now booming, but its present growth was preceded by over 20 years of stagnation. Its per capita GDP surpassed its 1981 level only in 2005.

In the 1950s, the GDP of Latin America was 25% that of the US, while Asia's was only 10%. But it was projected that they would catch up with America. They didn't. Today Asia's GDP is 25% that of the US, while Latin America has slipped to 20%.

In the 2008 crash, the S&P dropped 56%. A real disaster, but not bad compared with China and Russia. The Shanghai market hit its peak in October of 2007 at 6,058. Over the next year it plunged over 71%, until it hit bottom at 1,747. This is also not the first time it has plunged. Ten years ago, it fell from 2,125 in 2001 to 1,221 in 2006. Despite predictions of endless growth, the Chinese market is still only at half of its 2007 highs. In May 2011, the S&P recovered almost 90%. Russia has been even worse. Its stock market fell a stunning 77% in the crash. The Saudi stock market reached a high of 20,634 in 2006 and has never fully recovered. It is presently trading at 6,600, only 30% of its all-time high.

The judgment of sovereign debt has changed as well. The default swap market that presently smiles upon emerging markets was not always so forgiving. The cost of insuring Indonesia's sovereign debt in 2008 was 12.47% of the debt. Russia's cost was over 10% and Brazil's was over 5%.

One point that these statistics should make very clear is that these countries and their markets are like all countries and markets. They are very different from one another. For example, even a cursory look at the BRICs will reveal that they all have different political systems. India and Brazil have vibrant democracies. China and Russia are single-party states. China is the center of global trade. India is in many ways still removed from global trade. Both the Russian and Brazilian economies are heavily dependent on commodities that have soared recently, partially due to demand from China.

Rules: Game Changers

But perhaps the most important question to be asking about emerging markets is, why? Despite their rapid growth these countries remain very poor. For most of the twentieth century their growth was nonexistent. What has changed?

It's simple: the rules.

Even before these countries started to experience their rapid growth, they certainly had many of the factors of production, including land, cheap labor, and often abundant natural resources. What they lacked was the real magic necessary for sustainable economic growth—capital and entrepreneurship. It wasn't that there was something wrong with the culture. We have seen over the past five years that Indians can be just as hard-working and entrepreneurial as the Chinese. If given the appropriate incentives, people everywhere are willing to save money, even in the US.

The reason that these economies and many like them could not grow was because their governments would not let them. China, prior to opening up under Deng, was a Communist country, like Russia. India was restricted by the "License Raj." Eastern Europe was under the same oppressive system as Russia. Latin America was dominated by a series of military dictators. After price increases caused by the oil shock of 1973, Brazil suffered almost 20 years of high inflation and crushing foreign debt, mostly because of a detrimental industrial policy.

What changed was the legal infrastructure. Almost every one of these emerging markets once had a strongly socialist economy. In the 1990s, governments retreated from trying to manage the economy. State-owned industries were privatized. Regulations were trimmed or, in places like China, there were none at all. Foreign investments were encouraged. Taxes were simplified. Laws were modernized and clarified to protect private property rights.

The result was a boom in entrepreneurial activity and the formation of capital. The state no longer allocated capital. That job was left to the market. And many people who invested in these markets became very rich.

Investors Must Comprehend the Full Picture

But there is a dark side to the story. If, like Tom Friedman, you believe that globalization and the rise of the emerging markets is due to technology, then the trend cannot be reversed. No one is about to uninvent something. The same cannot be said about the rules. They can be changed at the stroke of a pen.

In some countries, the legal systems are indeed reforming. In other countries, the reverse is happening. In some emerging markets, the state is again growing and not shrinking as is generally assumed. As it does, it has the potential to kill economic growth.

The rest of this book will take a look at specific countries and the opportunities and pitfalls for investors. As we'll see, emerging markets do hold great promise. There is the potential for profitable investments, but a lot depends on where and when. There is no guarantee of consistent growth in all countries. To avoid the risks and pitfalls, it is important to understand the rules. If investors believe Wall Street's myth of constant continuous growth, they may find their bank accounts as empty as Chenggong.

Never Forget: You Are Not on Wall Street Anymore

Something is strange in my town. All of the nail salons are owned and staffed by Vietnamese people. Exactly why this has occurred is basic to the understanding of how emerging markets work.

The Vietnamese immigration to the United States occurred as an unforeseen consequence of the Vietnam War. After the fall of Saigon (now Ho Chi Minh City), many Vietnamese refugees ended up in camps in the United States. Many were well educated, but their skills were not always transferable, often because of their limited English language skills. American actress Tippi Hedren had the idea of teaching these refugees a simple skill that would allow them to make a living without being fluent in English. She flew her own manicurist in once a week to teach the women how to do manicures. Within a few months and with some additional education, the women were ready for work and became fully employed.[1]

---

[1] My-Thuan Tran, "A mix of luck, polish: Vietnamese dominance of the manicure trade started with the help of a U.S. star," *Los Angeles Times*, http://articles.latimes.com/2008/may/05/local/me-nails5, May 5, 2008.

The cost of a manicure at the time was over $60USD. Since the refugees were willing to work for less and there was, and still is, an additional supply of labor from immigration, the price for a manicure plummeted to around $15. Where I live, this service is still quite inexpensive. It still costs $15 for a regular manicure and $25 for the deluxe option.

But this is more than the story of hard-working immigrants being successful in a new country. Certainly, the Vietnamese ladies worked, and still work, long hours in a low-status manual trade. Certainly, they saved their money. Certainly, they used their money to support their families. But this is not, as some would say, the manifestation of culture or Asian Confucian virtue.

On the contrary, there is not even a word in the Vietnamese language for "manicurist" or "pedicurist." The expression they use is *tho nail*—nail worker.[2] From a cultural perspective, people in Vietnam who do hard manual labor or work with feet are near the bottom of the social hierarchy, just above people who dump garbage.[3] Undoubtedly, the provision of these services is a trade that requires little English, but there are many other similar trades. And it is not that Vietnamese immigrants just work as manicurists; they now dominate the business.

Vietnamese Americans make up an estimated 80% of manicurists in California and 43% in the rest of the United States. They have branched out beyond just manicures and pedicures to every aspect of the foot spa business. They dominate beauty product design and manufacturing for all products used in this industry—"[e]very spa chair, every nail tip, every color polish."[4]

So how did this happen? How did a particular group come to a different country and, within just a few decades, basically create an entire industry that they have come to control? The answer lies in their methods to accumulate capital, but fundamentally, it lies in game theory.

The Vietnamese people helped their business along by pooling their resources, forming loan clubs. From a legal perspective, these are partnerships. What happens is that a group of people come together and form an association. Every member or partner contributes a certain amount each week or month. The association then lends the money to its members. How the money is lent and to whom varies with the association. In some groups, the

[2] Ibid.

[3] Lynh Bui, "Foot in the Door: The pedicures might look pretty, but the American dream can turn ugly at the Valley's Vietnamese nail salons," *Phoenix New Times News*, www.phoenixnewtimes.com/2005-07-14/news/foot-in-the-door/, July 14, 2005.

[4] My-Thuan Tran, "A mix of luck, polish."

money is lent on a rotating basis, in others it is lent by chance in a lottery, and, in some, it goes by agreement to the neediest. Other associations use an auction. The person who promises the highest interest to the rest of the members gets the loan.

These informal banks are not exclusive to the Vietnamese community. They exist in many cultures. The Vietnamese refer to them as *hui* (associations). The Koreans call them *keh* (contracts). They have been very successful in helping the US Korean immigrant community match the success of the Vietnamese community in dominating the small grocery business in certain US cities. The Chinese refer to these banks as *biaohui;* they have been around for centuries. But it is not just the Asians who use these associations. The Caribbean community in the United States calls them *su-su* (among us or savings) and they are also widely used in Ghana. Mexican Americans call them *tandas* (turns).

These organizations experience the same major problem as any creditor or bank. Once they lend the money, how do they get repaid? The answer comes from game theory.

Rules vs. Relationships

In a normal game between a debtor and a lender, the debtor's best move is to not pay the money back. The lender knows this and so he doesn't lend. But as we know, lending goes on all the time. What forces debtors to honor their contracts and repay the loans? It depends on the system.

The one system that most people are familiar with is what Professor Avinash Dixit, in his book *Lawlessness and Economics,*[5] calls a rule-based system. This is a system based on rules or laws. In a rule-based system, the state acts as a neutral arbiter and enforces the law. If a contract for debt is considered proper according to the law of the jurisdiction, then a court will issue an order that allows the lender to utilize the enforcement powers of the state to collect the debt. The debtor repays the debt because there is a legal disincentive enforced by the state. Or to use the correct terminology, "[a] law that gives the Lender the ability to call upon the state to enforce its claim provides the parties with a way of transforming a game with a suboptimal equilibrium into another game with an optimal equilibrium."[6] Whew!

---

[5] Avinash K. Dixit, *Lawlessness and Economics: Alternative Modes of Governance* (Princeton, New Jersey, Princeton University Press, 2007).

[6] Douglas Baird, Robert Gertnmer, Randal Picker, *Game Theory and the Law* (Cambridge, MA: Harvard University Press, 1994).

Dixit also cites the relationship-based system. In this system, debtors repay debts because of *reputation*, as it is called in game theory. Reputation is based on the idea of repeated games. It is best illustrated by the expression, "fool me once, shame on you, fool me twice, shame on me." In one interaction, if a debtor refuses to repay the lender, without any possibility of state enforcement through law, the lender is basically out of luck. He cannot collect the debt. But what if there were several interactions? If the debtor knew that he might want to do business with the lender more than once, he would have a large incentive to pay the money back on time. The concept of reputation in repeated games gives the parties an incentive to cooperate.

For this process to function without punishment from the state, this system needs to be based on trust. And the most important factor for establishing trust is the existence of a relationship.

Relationships exist everywhere. They are, at some level, probably hardwired into our evolutionary biology. Humans are pack animals. We desperately need each other to survive; we have survived and succeeded because of our ability to work together.

Trust vs. Game Theory

These relationships are not only necessary for our survival, but they also make us feel good. The latest work of Nobel laureate Vernon Smith of George Mason University concerns the field of neuroeconomics. This field tests economic assumptions. He and other researchers do so by developing games. When the players play these games, their mental processes are monitored by functional magnetic resonance imaging (FMRI) brain scans. The researchers also measure pulse rates, skin conductivity, and hormone levels.

They played a game called the "trust game." The rules of the game are as follows: The researchers give a player $10. The player has two choices. He/she can keep the money or give it away to an anonymous person that the player has never met. If the player-donor gives the money away to the anonymous beneficiary, he/she knows that the money will be quadrupled to $40 in the beneficiary's hands. Now the beneficiary also has a choice; he/she has $40. The player can keep the whole $40 or give the original donor $15 back. The beneficiary has no reason to share his/her good fortune.

According to game theory, a game like this between two unrelated players would not result in any donation. The player-donor would not take the risk. His/her best move would be to keep the money. But this is not what real players do. The researchers found that half of the player-donors took the risk. More than half were rewarded, because over three-quarters of their anonymous beneficiaries were kind enough to return the favor and send some money back. The player-donor's trust was rewarded.

The brain scans showed something very interesting. The player-donors who took the risk were shown to use parts of their brain called Brodman's areas 8 and 10. These areas are associated with thinking about others; in this case, trying to determine the motivations of other players. They are also associated with the process of delaying gratification to receive higher rewards later. The brains of players who decided not to donate or players who were playing against a computer rather than an anonymous beneficiary did not use these areas of their brains.

But it is not just specific areas of the brain that show activity. The levels of certain neuropeptides rise as well. Our brains produce a number of hormones that affect our moods. One such hormone is oxytocin. When stimulated, oxytocin elevates your mood. It makes you feel good. Oxytocin is usually associated with reproduction. It is produced by new mothers, allowing them to lactate. It also can be stimulated by eating, massage, and sex. Professor Paul Zak of Claremont University found that it could also be stimulated by social signals, such as being trusted.

So when we trust, we feel good. But whom do we trust? Obviously, our earliest trust is the family, our group, our pack. In time, we learn to trust other people. These are usually people in our tribe or our network—people with whom we have a certain commonality, members of our ethnic group, members of our religion, members of the same political party, people who speak our language, and those who share our values. These are people with whom we can develop a relationship.

Socializing Highlights Incentives and Disincentives

It is hardly surprising, then, that savings associations are not only business enterprises but also social groups. Each gathering of a keh, notes Sungsoo Kim, president of the Korean-American Small Business Center of New York, is a "great party with food and drinks and everything." Aurora Lares, who owns a Mexican restaurant with her brother in Santa Monica, says, "A tanda is for helping people and for making good friends."[7]

---

[7] Christine Gorman, "Do-It-Yourself Financing," *Time,* www.time.com/time/magazine/article/0,9171,967966,00.html, July 25, 1988.

Socializing has two other benefits for a relationship-based system. It helps the members keep an eye on each other. Obviously, every member of the group has a financial incentive to watch the other members of the group in order to lower the asymmetry of information that is part of any debtor-lender relationship. So the gossip and conversations that are part of the bonding rituals increase trust by increasing information. They also provide a wealth of experience to help similar businesses.

The second use of socializing is to provide a disincentive. Without state-provided disincentives, punishment must be severe. Any member of the group who does not pay back the money risks not only financial loss, but the possibility of being ostracized by the group. Any damage to their reputation could reverse all of the benefits of being part of a community.

In New York, there is a tightly knit community of Jewish diamond merchants. They make deals worth hundreds of thousands of dollars using only a handshake. Even in a country like the United States where laws are ubiquitous, the use of courts is avoided. Instead, transactions are enforced by the need to maintain one's reputation in the community. If you lose your reputation, you are out of business, and out of the community.

Relation-based systems do not just exist in modern times. They are a type of prelaw-based system. In places where the state could not enforce debts or other contracts, people had to rely on the disincentives inherent in relation-based systems. Many were neither small nor local. When the Medicis started their international banking empire in the fifteenth century, they did not have faxes or telephones. Transporting money was very slow and dangerous. They could do business if all they had to send was worthless paper. But for the paper to substitute for money, for it to have value, it had to be backed with something valuable, in this case trust. The Medicis were able to trade across great distances because they had a family network. They did not need laws because they had trusted relationships based on family. They knew that the bills of exchange sent to other cities would be honored. If any family member broke that trust, they were not only out of the business, they were out of the family.

The Chinese diaspora throughout Southeast Asia has, over time, created enormously profitable commercial networks. These networks have one thing in common. The members of the network can all trace their lineage back to a single Chinese village in the province of Fujian. They also spoke a dialect of Mandarin called Hokkien.

Each member of the network has established a relationship with his trading partners and the network is aware of each member's reputation. The Southeast Asian trading networks, says the *Financial Times*, developed "an onion-like structure of 'relatedness,' ranging from the nuclear family to the ethnic group of Hokkien-Chinese to Non-Chinese, associated with declining levels of trustworthiness."[8] These networks were incredibly successful. Descendants of the Hokkien-Chinese today dominate the economic life in Malaysia, Singapore, Thailand, Indonesia, the Philippines, Taiwan, and Thailand.

Microfinance Made Possible through Relationships

The relationships associated with lending have a very modern application, microfinance. Microfinance was developed to provide the poor with access to capital. With little education, few assets to use as security, uneven incomes, and perhaps not even proximity to a traditional bank, the poor in all countries have little or no way to borrow money. This gap is often filled by moneylenders or loan sharks who routinely charge interest in excess of 100% per year, and sometimes even over 1000%. Moneylenders and loan sharks cannot often rely on the state, and so provide their own "muscle" to enforce the contracts.

Microfinance relies on the social disincentives of relationships. Money is loaned to a single individual, but often a group, usually women, is collectively responsible for the debt. Women have a much lower delinquency rate, most likely because the relationships between groups of women are stronger. This may be due to evolutionary biology. Recent studies have shown that female baboons "with a strong, supportive social network are healthier and have greater reproductive success."[9]

Relationship-based systems are a type of prelaw system. The laws in Renaissance Italy certainly did exist and courts were available, but the reach of the state was limited. Trade throughout Southeast Asia and, even very recently, most of global trade had very little law at all. The only system that businesspeople could rely on was a relationship-based system. The same is true of immigrant communities. Anyone finding themselves with no money in an alien land without language skills or connections cannot build the type of trust needed to do business.

Most emerging markets face exactly the same issues. If we just limit ourselves to the BRIC countries, we will see a common thread of weak institutions.

---

[8] Tim Harford, "In search of the inside story of economics," *Financial Times*, www.ft.com, September 29, 2003.

[9] Joan B. Silk, Jacinta C. Beehner, Thore J. Bergman, Catherine Crockford, Anne L. Engh, Liza R. Moscovice, Roman M. Wittig, Robert M. Seyfarth, and Dorothy L. Cheney. "Strong and Consistent Social Bonds Enhance the Longevity of Female Baboons," *Current Biology*, www.cell.com/current-biology/retrieve/pii/S0960982210007219, July 1, 2010.

None of these countries can escape their unfortunate histories. Russia has not shaken off its communist past and China, despite the PR, is still a communist country. The central governments in both countries have dominated both the economic and the political systems. There is no room for independent institutions like courts or effective legislatures. All of the power comes from a single party with only self-preservation and self-interest as guiding lights. The result is that any and all aspects of business and investment can be changed at any time. Any investment, any business, is basically a calculated bet on the future. If the future legal framework can be changed at any time to suit the needs of the party, you have to rely on something else.

India is a little better, but it is barely emerging from years of socialist rule. Until 1992, it was stifled by an endless bureaucracy known as the "License Raj." Although large parts of the process have been dismantled, much of it, including labor laws that prevent India from providing jobs for her billions of poor, still remain. It has a great legacy in British common law, but its court system is so hopelessly jammed that laws are totally ineffective.

Brazil did not have either a communist or a socialist state, but the state did, and still does, interfere with its markets. The idea of state-led development should have been buried years ago, but it is still alive and well.

All systems provide different incentives and disincentives. The point is that they are different. The rules that exist in relationship-based systems are perhaps not as clear as those from rule-based systems, but that does not mean they do not exist. The framework created by a relationship-based system has created certain hallmarks that investors will find in all emerging markets. To do business or invest in these markets, it is important to know how and why these systems work the way they do, because the rules that apply to developed markets, such as those that apply on Wall Street or in the City, don't necessarily translate.

Family Affairs

One would expect that in a relationship-based system, in which relationships are crucial to doing business, families would be important—and they certainly are. This is prevalent in all emerging markets. In Asia, families control almost two-thirds of the 1,000 largest companies. In Hong Kong alone, over 70% of the listed companies are controlled either by their founders, or by members of the founder's family.[10]

---

[10] Robert Cookson, "Learning to play the corporate generation game," *Financial Times*, www.ft.com, January 26, 2011.

South Korea is another example. South Korea is dominated by several dozen large family-owned corporate groups, generally referred to as *chaebols*. They dominate the most important part of the South Korean economy, the export sector, which represents 43% of the GDP. Small- to medium-size firms are relegated to the service sector, which has, in fact, shrunk from 55.8% of the economy to 52.5%.[11]

The heads of these chaebols have a long history of behaving badly. For example, Lee Kun-hee, the chairman of Samsung Electronics and South Korea's richest man, was convicted of tax evasion, but the conviction was expunged. Lee Kun-hee is hardly unique. South Korea's president, Lee Myung-bak, recently pardoned 74 top executives.[12]

In essence, the power of these firms extends throughout the economy. It is not only their personal connections. They have extended their power by careful hiring. A study by the People's Solidarity for Participatory Democracy (PSPD), a human rights organization, cited 278 individuals who had been employed by Samsung. The list includes "101 who were formerly bureaucrats, including an ex-prime minister, and 87 former academicians, 59 executives with career backgrounds in the legal profession, including 28 former prosecutors, 22 former judges, 3 Supreme Court judges, 27 with backgrounds in journalism, 22 former economists, 13 former politicians, 13 certified public accountants, seven former culture artists and six former social activists."[13]

Indonesia's most powerful family-run conglomerate is the Bakrie group. The Bakries made their fortune under the authoritarian Suharto regime, lost it in the 1997-98 Asian financial crisis that toppled the regime, and then restored their riches under the wobbly democratic governments that followed.

The Bakries have retained their influence to this day in the present government. The head of the family, Aburizal Bakrie, is the elected leader of a majority parliamentary coalition with President Susilo Bambang Yudhoyono's party.

In mid-2008, with commodities riding high, the group's holding company, Bakrie & Brothers, took out $1.4 billion in loans. Then came the credit

---

[11] Christian Oliver, "Seoul tells chaebol sharks to leave small fry," *Financial Times*, www.ft.com, August 14, 2011.

[12] "Pardon Me? Pardons for corporate criminals in South Korea," *The Economist*, www.economist.com/node/16693589?story_id=16693589, July 29, 2010.

[13] Kim Sung-jin, "Samsung Bashing Corners Chairman: Korea's Leading Conglomerate Beset by Allegations of Buying Political Influence, Recruiting Lobbyists," *Korea Times*, www.koreatimes.co.kr/, May 8, 2005.

crunch and the collapse in commodities. In six months' time, the Bakrie empire went from $8.2 billion to less than a billion, and it could not guarantee the loans. Defaults began and triggered a meltdown on the Jakarta stock market, forcing its closure for three days. By 2009, the Bakries had rebounded, disposing of more than $1.1 billion in debt. The rest of the empire, which includes mobile telecoms, plantations, energy, and property, remains intact. How the Bakries were able to accomplish such a miracle is only speculation. But no doubt they had a little help from their friends—including the ones in government.

India created thousands of new firms since the License Raj was trimmed. By 2005, there were 8,864 firms less than 20 years old, which required the filing of financial statements amounting to 56% of the total. The problem is that they accounted for only 15% of corporate assets, 17% of sales, and 13% of profits. The rest of the economy, about 75%, is in the hands of state firms or large family-controlled groups that dominate the Sensex index.[14]

The most colorful example of the Indian family firm and elements of crony capitalism is the Ambani family. Its founder, Dhirubhai Ambani, is the subject of a book by Hamish McDonald, who wrote *The Polyester Prince* in 1998.[15] According to Mr. McDonald, "Indians complain that social connections trump hard work. But no one worked harder than Dhirubhai at forging connections. His philosophy was to cultivate everybody from the doorkeeper up. With the help of these relationships, Reliance set about making the most of India's famous 'License Raj.'"

Family Connects with Government

China has its own form of aristocrats. These are the "princelings," descendants of China's revolutionary founders. They hold the highest political offices in China. "[With a] Politburo reshuffle in 2007," writes *The Economist*, "princelings have occupied seven out of 25 seats, up from three in 2002."[16] It appears that the next Paramount Leader of China will be Xi Jinping, a princeling. Besides political office, the only offices that count in China, these princelings are also heads of many corporate entities. Princelings include

---

[14] "Dancing elephants: Is Indian capitalism becoming oligarchic?" *The Economist*, www.economist.com/node/18010749, January 27, 2011.

[15] Hamish McDonald, *The Polyester Prince: The Rise of Dhirubhai Ambani* (Australia: Allen & Unwin, Limited, 1999).

[16] "China's new rulers: Princelings and the goon state: The rise and rise of the princelings, the country's revolutionary aristocracy," *The Economist*, www.economist.com/node/18561005?story_id=18561005, April 14, 2011.

"President Hu Jintao's son, Hu Haifeng, who headed a big provider of airport scanners; and Wen Yunsong, a financier who is the son of Wen Jiabao, the prime minister."[17] They even have their own society, the Beijing Friendship Association of the Sons and Daughters of Yan'an, a sort of Daughters of the American Revolution (DAR) for Chinese communist revolutionary spawn, but with a lot more power and better connections.

The oligarchs of Russia are certainly prime examples of family firms, but since Putin's rise to power, they are not the source of real power. Presently, the real source of power is another class of elites. They are Russia's *siloviki* or "strong guys." Their connection to Prime Minister Putin and each other are mainly the security services, basically KGB and its descendants. The siloviki in Russia are more like those in China in that they owe their power to the old communist régime and not to the market economy. Like the Chinese, their instincts are in favor of state control of the economy.

The siloviki are generally considered to be divided into two "clans," mostly for administrative purposes in dividing up the spoils. According to the *Financial Times*, They "hit their apogee in 2007, when they accounted for two out of every three members of the president's administration. But following the accession to the presidency of Dmitry Medvedev, they are this year down to barely one in two."[18]

Even Israel, which has all of the trappings of a developed sophisticated market, is dominated by family firms. "Prices for Israeli consumers and businesses are high because a handful of politically well-connected families control the economy through monopolistic conglomerates."[19]

Implications for Investors

The point for investors about families in emerging markets is crucial. I remember a story told by a corporate counsel many years ago. Two firms were competing for a contract in Saudi Arabia, an American firm and a Japanese firm. The American firm flew in their CEO, the division chief, and the corporate counsel for several days of negotiations. When these people arrived, they discovered that the Japanese had a twenty-strong delegation that had been there for three weeks.

---

[17] Ibid.

[18] Charles Clover, "Russia: Shift to the shadows," *Financial Times*, www.ft.com, December 16, 2009.

[19] "Indignant in Israel," *Financial Times*, www.ft.com, August 11, 2011.

The Japanese, who are from a system that tilts to the relationship end of the spectrum, understood that, to do business, it is necessary to take the time to develop the appropriate relationships. Or, as Professor Avinash Dixit points out in his book, "An investor from a rule-based system who lends to someone in a relation-based system without developing the necessary relationship in advance is asking to be robbed."[20]

The direct investor must understand that no matter how modern and sophisticated his counterpart may seem—many have been educated at the best schools in Europe and the United States—he is still doing business with an old-school patriarchal family firm. He should understand that power does not lie with the nominal CEO or with the board but with Papa, if he is still alive, or the head of the family. If you do not have, or at least attempt to develop, a relationship with the family, your deal may not be what you expect regardless of what that expensive contract says.

Indirect investors must also be aware of the limitations of corporate governance. Even though the family's share of the business might have become quite small, you can be sure that it is still controlling. The prime directive of these businesses is to protect the family's interests. In countries like Russia and China, the interests are often political. If their interests coincide with the interests of the passive or foreign shareholders, then well and good. If not, it is not their problem. To protect yourself, but still profit from the growth, an Exchange-Traded Fund (ETF) might be a better idea than stock picking.

Neither direct nor indirect investors should have illusions about finding relief in the courts. It is not that the local courts are always corrupt or useless in emerging markets. Depending on the country, some are becoming quite proficient, but they are not necessarily the independent neutral institutions that might exist at home. Even in the United States, the federal court system was established specifically to prevent local prejudice from influencing justice for litigants from other states. There are more ways to influence a judge than with just money. If you are going to invest in a country, be sure that you are playing by their rules. It is far better to have the local system working in your favor.

Underground Economies

The Republic of Venice can trace its founding back to the eighth century. It was a proud, independent republic that relied on a complex set of laws to

---

[20] Avinash Dixit, *Lawlessness and Economics: Alternative Modes of Governance* (Princeton, New Jersey, Princeton University Press, 2004), p. 84.

successfully govern itself for almost a thousand years. Florence and other city states in Tuscany were also very successful independent republics for centuries. Even when the city's government reverted to an inherited autocracy controlled by the Medici, at least they were ruled by locals and local laws.

The south of Italy, the Mezzogiorno, had no such luck. Its history is one of continuous foreign occupation. The Byzantines, Lombards, Arabs, Normans, Germans, French, Austrians, Spanish, and even Napoleon conquered either Naples, Sicily, or both. Ruled by foreign, often absentee, landlords whose laws could be both capacious and unfair, the locals developed their own relationship-based system that depended both on family connections and often forced the provision of structure.

These systems are quite famous, since they followed Sicilians and Neapolitans when they migrated to the United States. These are the regions' Mafias, including the Sicilian Cosa Nostra, Neapolitan Camorra, the Apulian Sacra Corona Unita, and the Calabrian 'Ndrangheta. Although law enforcement in Italy has made some progress in reasserting the law, the 'Ndrangheta has expanded from its traditional base. "Police operations show that the 'Ndrangheta from Calabria has burrowed deep into the economic fabric of the north."[21]

These criminal organizations are evidence of the effect of law in emerging markets. When the legal infrastructure provided by the state is weak, capricious, biased, or delayed, people seek alternatives. If the law imposes too many burdens on an economy, as in irrational regulations or pervasive fees, they will simply be ignored or not paid. Often, it is not the regulations themselves that create the problems. It is the people enforcing them. If regulations require constantly escalating payments to rent-seeking bureaucrats, businesses will find it easier to do business outside the system.

In strong relationship-based systems, the best way to work outside the system is with people you trust. The people you trust are often in your family. The idea that the various Mafias are crime families is a very accurate description and applies to underground economies throughout emerging markets.

The causes of weak institutions are many and varied. Sometimes, it is a history of foreign occupation that hobbled legal institutions. Authoritarian governments do not like their power to be limited by law. Even democratic governments can stray beyond the normal role of government to protect and educate citizens and attempt to control markets through pervasive, intrusive regulatory environments required for a socialist or command economy.

---

[21] "Sounder public finances, but a weaker economy: that is Italy today," *The Economist,* www.economist.com/node/18530672?story_id=18530672, April 7, 2011.

Black Market Riches

Every country in the world has an underground economy. They differ only by degree, and they are particularly pervasive in emerging markets. Although underground or informal economies are more insidious in emerging markets, they certainly exist in developed countries as well. In a recent poll of the European Union's 27 members, almost 30% of some of its most honest citizens, the Danes and the Dutch, admitted to paying for unlicensed, unregistered, or illegal goods and services.[22]

The most accurate measure of a legal infrastructure's efficiency is the size of its underground economy. In most of the OECD countries, the estimated size is about 13.8% of the GDP. Of course, this varies widely. Greece has an estimated black economy that represents 25% of its GDP. Italy's is 22%. The illegal economy in the United States, Switzerland, and Austria represent only 7.6%, 8.3%, and 8.5% of their GDPs, respectively.[23]

While the underground economy in the United States seems relatively small compared to other countries, that does not mean it is irrelevant. The reported US GDP is close to $14 trillion. This means that a trillion dollar grey or black economy goes unreported and untaxed. It escapes economic and financial forecasts. It does not come within the purview of government or private company plans or programs.

As this problem is multiplied from country to country across the world, we start to see major distortions. Greece misses out on €15 billion of revenue annually. The Italian tax authority loses €100 billion. Both Greece and Italy are relatively sophisticated developed countries.[24]

The less-developed and emerging markets make up far more of the world's economy than ever before. As these economies have grown, so has the size of their subterranean economies, which leaves an ever larger hole in accurate information.

One obvious example is China. China's capricious regulations and state-dominated economy guarantee a large grey economy. It is so large that it dwarfs the economies of many countries. But China's secretive markets are

---

[22] "The underground economy: A grey area," *The Economist*, www.economist.com/node/10050118?story_id=E1_TDDVDTTR, October 29, 2007.

[23] Alistair Gray, "Tax dodgers prove robust in hard times," *Financial Times*, www.ft.com, November 20, 2010.

[24] "Tax evasion: Dues and don'ts: Southern Europe will have trouble increasing its tax take," *The Economist*, August 12, 2010.

not just about simple illegal activities. They include all forms of finance. The alternative banking system in China comes in various forms. According to former *Financial Times* Beijing correspondent James Kynge, they include "off-balance-sheet lending by state banks, the funds under management by 'private' funds and the assets of a booming multitude of unregistered banks and loan sharks."[25]

According to Mr. Kynge, the total amount of lending in this underground financial system could top an estimated 6 trillion renminbi.[26] If this amount is added to the reported loans of 7 trillion renminbi, you end up with a money supply that is out of control and certainly heading toward inflation.

But China is definitely not alone. Informal economies in developing countries average about 41% of the economy.[27] The percentage of workers employed in the informal sector is even higher. "[I]nformal employment makes up 48% of non-agricultural employment in North Africa, 51% in Latin America, 65% in Asia, and 72% in sub-Saharan Africa. If agricultural employment is included, the percentages rise, in some countries like India and many sub-Saharan African countries beyond 90%."[28]

Crony Capitalism and Corruption

With powerful family groups and large underground economies, can crony capitalism and corruption be far behind? The term crony capitalism originated during the Asian financial crisis of 1997. It is a system where business success is more dependent upon connections with high government officials than with entrepreneurial ability. For most of the 1990s, many economists, financial analysts, and investors treated the Asian "Tiger" countries (South Korea, Taiwan, Hong Kong, Thailand, and Malaysia) with a reverence that is today reserved for BRIC countries. All that came to an end with the collapse of the Thai baht in July 1997. To explain the collapse of economies that had been hailed as a new and more perfect model for rapid economic growth, economists created this pejorative term where a supposedly moral failure was the cause of their bad predictions.

---

[25] James Kynge, "China's twilight economy boosts inflation," *Financial Times*, www.ft.com, November 21, 2010.

[26] Ibid.

[27] "In the shadows: The informal economy is neither small nor benign," *The Economist*, www.economist.com/node/2766310, June 17, 2004.

[28] "Informal sector," Wikipedia, http://en.wikipedia.org/wiki/Informal_sector#cite_note-ilo-4, (PDF) Men and Women in the Informal Economy. International Labour Organisation. 2002. ISBN 92-2-113103-3. Retrieved December 18, 2006.

The reality is that enterprises, usually family enterprises, are simply trying to exploit a competitive advantage through the use of their connections and relationships. The problem with crony capitalism is that these connections are invariably connected to a government. It is the government that distorts the market. It is the politicians who take the bribes and kickbacks.

Crony capitalism is sort of anti-antitrust. It exists when the government itself colludes to decrease competition, which eventually hinders growth of the entire economy. For example, in India the majority of Indian firms still operate in industries that would be deemed "concentrated" by the standards of America's antitrust authorities.

Another flagrant example of crony capitalism occurred recently in the Indian telecom industry. At the time, Andimuthu Raja headed the Indian telecom ministry. Mr. Raja apparently had three qualifications for the job. He was loyal to the politically crucial Dravida Munnetra Kazhagam, or D.M.K., a regional party based in Tamil Nadu. He also had a close relationship with Kanimozhi, the daughter of the D.M.K. leader, Mr. Karunanidhi. Finally, he was no threat to anyone.

As minister, he was in charge of a 2008 auction that sold valuable mobile telephone spectrum licenses. Eight of the new telecom licenses were sold to domestic companies for a total of about $2 billion. These companies then turned around and sold stakes to large international telecom firms like Telenor of Norway and Etisalat of the UAE. An investigation started in 2009 has resulted in charges that the licenses were sold at prices that cost the Indian government about $39 billion in lost license revenue.

As part of the investigation, several of India's best known tycoons, including Anil Ambani, chairman of Reliance ADAG (son of Dhirubhai Ambani), Prashant Ruia, the billionaire chief executive of Essar Group, and distinguished chairman of the Tata Group, Ratan Tata, have been questioned by either the Central Bureau of Investigation or by a parliamentary committee to determine their involvement. It is a perfect example of several powerful families using their government connections to acquire, for themselves or for their firms, competitive advantage at public expense—in other words, crony capitalism.

But it is not only Asia that uses large family-owned company connections to dominate the economy. One of the worst examples is the power exercised in Mexico by Carlos Slim. Carlos Slim is one of the world's richest men. Through his company, Telmex, he operates 92% of all fixed phone lines in

Mexico.[29] His virtual monopoly of land lines has remained strong due to his ability to use his connections to create and protect his empire. A decades-long antitrust lawsuit went nowhere.

The only reason his hold on land lines has weakened is because of technology and a fortunate bit of legislation. Barred from television, Telmex has been unable to offer the "triple play" where cable providers offer telephone, the Internet, and television.

His land lines business was further weakened by a 1999 law, whereby mobile customers receive calls free of charge. This allowed mobile usage to increase 900% while fixed-line service in the country stagnated. Of course, Slim was not at a total loss; his mobile phone company, America Movile, controls 77% of the mobile market.

The Indian and Mexican telecom markets are examples of the tightly woven fabric of the relationships between powerful families and governments that persists throughout emerging markets. They are, of course, mutually beneficial. The families take the profits in exchange for bribes and kickbacks. The evidence of this is the level of corruption that exists in all emerging markets. According to the Transparency International Corruption Perception Index, none of the BRICS even make it into the top third. China at 78 and India at 87 barely make it into the top half, while Russia is down in the bottom quarter, tied with five African countries. The "stars" are Brazil at 69 and South Africa at 54.[30]

No Incentive to Change

Contrary to many assumptions about emerging markets, the problems of crony capitalism and corruption do not necessarily get better with economic growth. China's rank between 2009 and 2010 remained about the same. Brazil did improve but both India and Russia got worse.

The reason is simple. There is often no economic reason to clean up corruption. The system works very well for those fortunate individuals who are plugged into the system. If, as a local businessperson, you can make a fortune on local monopolies that lessen competition, especially from potentially more efficient foreign firms, you naturally will use any competitive advantage at your disposal.

---

[29] "Mexico's government gets tougher on monopolists," *The Economist,* www.economist.com/node/10235372?story_id=E1_TDNPVPSN, November 30, 2007.

[30] Transparency International Corruption Perceptions Index 2010, Transparency International, www.transparency.org/policy_research/surveys_indices/cpi/2010/results.

For politicians and bureaucrats in single-party states, there is little fear of any accountability from the electorate. Since they control the enforcement mechanisms, like the prosecutors and courts, there is little fear of punishment. In countries like Russia, China, and many other emerging markets, another major disincentive, a free press filled with hard-working investigative journalists, can usually be silenced. So with huge economic incentives and few legal disincentives, there are no limits to the potential plunder. Economic growth only increases the takings, especially if foreign investors are eager and willing to add to the pot.

For direct investors in emerging markets, corruption presents an insidious problem. Often the glue that holds relationships together has to do with favors and bribes. Obviously, the beneficiaries of the bribes, government officials, are in no hurry to cut off a lucrative source of income not only for themselves but for their party members and families.

For example, the Organization for Economic Co-operation and Development and the Asian Development Bank have created an anti-corruption initiative with 28 Asia-Pacific governments. All of the governments have laws that make it illegal to bribe their own officials with money, but there are some huge gaps. Often the legislation is drafted narrowly with various exclusions, such as payments for third parties, like tuition for children. Certain classes of government officials are excluded, like legislators, judges, and local government officials.[31] Only 8 of the 28 countries have made it illegal for their citizens to bribe foreigners. So it is not a crime for citizens of China, India, and Indonesia to bribe citizens in another country.[32] According to research by Trace, a US non-profit association that tracks cross-border corruption, "10 Asian countries [are] among the world's top 34 bribe-taking locations, with China and Indonesia in fourth and fifth places."[33] Even with laws, prosecution and real punishment are virtually nonexistent and corporate liability only theoretical.

In contrast, the threat of corporate and personal liability for companies from developed countries, such as the United States and the United Kingdom, are becoming very real. In the United States, the Foreign Corrupt Practices Act (FCPA) was originally passed in the 1970s. It was passed as a result of a bribe paid by Lockheed to a Japanese politician for preference in a defense contract. Since 1981, there have been 118 US cases involving 242

---

[31] Kevin Brown, "Time for Asia to wage its own war on corruption," *Financial Times*, www.ft.com., March 15, 2011.

[32] Ibid.

[33] Ibid.

companies and about 167 prosecutions.[34] Only 3% of investigations have resulted in no action. For many years, it was rarely used, but now the US Justice Department considered its enforcement to be second only to fighting terrorism in terms of priority. "The number of investigations launched each year has been steadily increasing, from five in 2004 to 56 last year, and at least 150 companies are currently subject to inquiries."[35]

This situation is not only occurring in American firms. The German engineering company, Siemens AG, has been forced to pay an $800 million fine, and Alcatel-Lucent, the French telecoms group, agreed to pay a $137 million fine. As emerging market firms grow and come under US jurisdiction, they are being targeted as well. The Indian multinational, Tata Communications, has disclosed that it is presently under investigation.[36] Despite US efforts, it is unlikely that the unequal situation regarding corruption will change any time soon.

Implications for Investors

For indirect investors, the problem of corruption must be considered in the analysis of any emerging market company. Often the success of these companies is attributed to savvy business practices, but more likely, it is due to unsavory business practices. This does not mean that these companies will not be profitable. Often this competitive advantage can reap rewards. But the problem with corruption is that, by definition, it will not surface in any press release, SEC disclosure, or company report. Corrupt officials can be rented but not bought. So the success of a company in one quarter may disappear in the next as another competitor with better connections and more cash makes a better offer. The result is that time frames in emerging markets have to be kept short. A corrupt environment makes forecasts even more problematic as certainty declines.

State-owned Companies

Family-owned companies are not the only types of companies that are prevalent in emerging markets. State-owned companies also dominate certain economies and markets.

---

[34] Brian Groom, "Bribery legislation warning for energy groups," *Financial Times*, www.ft.com, May 8, 2011.

[35] Kevin Brown, "Time for Asia to wage its own war on corruption." *Financial Times*, www.ft.com, March 15, 2011.

[36] Ibid.

China is supposed to be the home of a billion capitalists. According to the National Bureau of Statistics, there are "40 million or so small and medium-size enterprises—which employ at least 75% of China's workers and produce 68% of industrial output."[37] They are responsible for 68% of China's exports, 66% of the country's patent applications, and more than 80% of its new products.[38]

Despite their dominance in many things, smaller companies are definitely second-class citizens in China. Large companies are supposed to make up one-third of the companies in China, but the reality is that no one really knows if this is the case. As *The Economist* tells us, "Chinese firms fall into a bewildering variety of legal categories."[39] Corporate records are often secret and may not reveal the true shareholders even if they were open.

What is true is that they probably make up all of the listed companies. Certainly, the largest companies are. The 20 biggest stocks on China's market include 12 state-owned financial firms and three state-owned energy companies.[40] Financial firms alone make up 28% of Shanghai's market capitalization.[41] Allowing private companies to list is contrary to the purpose of China's stock market. State-owned companies anywhere are usually poorly managed because there is no incentive for profit. The managers are usually political hacks. So they often lose money. Allowing them to list gives them access to cheap capital.

Private companies in China are regarded with suspicion. During the recent slowdown, Chinese state-owned banks were required to make massive loans as part of a stimulus package. In the United States, the stimulus package was a mere $780 billion. If the US stimulus package was as large as the Chinese stimulus relative to its GDP, it would have been over $6 trillion. But this wall of money never went near smaller private business. Most of it

---

[37] Jason Leow, "China Loans Hard to Get: Smaller Enterprises Left Dry as Bulk of Lending Goes to Big Projects," *The Wall Street Journal*, http://online.wsj.com/article/SB124224220005416213.html, May 14, 2009.

[38] "China's struggling smaller firms: Small fish in a big pond," *The Economist*, www.economist.com/node/14409584?story_id=E1_TQQDJVRQ, September 10, 2009.

[39] "Entrepreneurship in China: Let a million flowers bloom," *The Economist*, www.economist.com/node/18330120?story_id=18330120, March 10, 2011.

[40] James T. Areddy, "China Stocks Could Be Hindered in 2008 by Slower Profit Growth," *Wall Street Journal*, http://online.wsj.com/article/SB119930118784462727.html, January 3, 2008.

[41] Pan Qing, "Shanghai bourse launches financial stock index," *China Economic Review*, www.chinaeconomicreview.com/dailybriefing/2007_11_26/Shanghai_bourse_launches_financial_stock_index.html, November 26, 2007.

went to large state-owned firms or local governments. Less than 10% was allocated to smaller firms.[42]

China is hardly alone in its dominance of state-owned firms. According to Indonesia's State-owned Enterprises minister, Mustafa Abubakar, "Currently, 40 percent of our gross domestic product (GDP) comes from state-owned enterprises."[43] Vietnam has the same concentration. According to the official released figures, the leading state-owned enterprises (SOEs) make up nearly 40% of the GDP.[44]

In Brazil, the two largest companies, the oil giant Petrobras and the mining company, Vale, are both controlled by the state and make up 26% of the market capitalization of the Bovespa.[45] Two large state-owned banks dominate Brazil's finances. Banco do Brazil is the country's biggest financial firm, with a fifth of total assets,[46] and the National Bank for Economic and Social Development (BNDES) accounts for 40% of the lending.[47]

Despite mass privatizations in the 1990s, the Russian state still owns large sectors of the economy. Federal and regional governments control about 40% of the stock market capitalization. These include various sectors: banking represents 64% of the market capitalization, oil and gas 47%, and utilities 37%. In addition to the partially state-owned listed companies, the Russian state owns full control of 19.2% of the manufacturing industry, 15.3% of the fuel production, 11.6% of the metallurgy industry, and 25.7% of the chemical industry.[48]

---

[42] "China's struggling smaller firms: Small fish in a big pond," *The Economist.* http://www.economist.com/node/14409584?story_id=14409584, September 10, 2009.

[43] Rangga D. Fadillah, "SOEs' net profits expected to reach Rp 113.72t this year," *The Jakarta Post*, www.thejakartapost.com/news/2011/01/28/soes%E2%80%99-net-profits-expected-reach-rp-11372t-year.html, January 28, 2011.

[44] "Leading SOEs make up 40 percent of GDP?" *Vietnam Financial News*, www.vietfinancenews.com/2011/02/leading-soes-make-up-40-percent-of-gdp.html, February 28, 2011.

[45] ETF Report, http://etfreport.blogspot.com/2011/01/investing-in-huge-brazilian-boom.html, January 4, 2011.

[46] "The bigger and bigger picture: The developing world's banks are flourishing," *The Economist*, www.economist.com/node/16078500?story_id=E1_TGDSRVDD, May 13, 2010.

[47] "Brazil's development bank: Nest egg or serpent's egg? Ahead of presidential elections, BNDES comes under scrutiny," *The Economist*, www.economist.com/node/16748990?story_id=16748990, August 5, 2010.

[48] Carsten Spranger, "State Owned Enterprises in Russia," www.oecd.org/dataoecd/23/31/42576825.pdf, October 27, 2008.

In India, 246 enterprises are owned by the state. They employed almost 1.6 million people in 2008.[49] There are more than 40 public enterprises already listed on India's stock markets and these account for 37% of sales. The largest portion of sales, 47%, is by India's large, older family-owned companies.[50]

Financial Behemoths—and Growing

State-owned companies are not just small local companies. The largest corporations anywhere are in emerging markets.

> The 13 largest energy companies on Earth, measured by the reserves they control, are now owned and operated by governments. Saudi Aramco, Gazprom (Russia), China National Petroleum Corp., National Iranian Oil Co., Petróleos de Venezuela, Petrobras (Brazil), and Petronas (Malaysia) are all larger than ExxonMobil, the largest of the multinationals. Collectively, multinational oil companies produce just 10% of the world's oil and gas reserves. State-owned companies now control more than 75% of all crude oil production.[51]

Governments in emerging markets are not content with just owning the corporations; they feel that they should invest national wealth as well. Rather than returning the wealth to their population, either directly or through improvements in infrastructure, they created Sovereign Wealth Funds. With the exception of the Alaska Permanent Fund and the Norway Government Pension Fund, these funds are all in emerging markets. Most of them invest oil money, but the notable exceptions are China and Singapore. Together they control almost $2.5 trillion. They may make up only 2% of the world's $165 trillion-worth of listed securities, but the power is concentrated in a few hands. The funds in emerging markets are neither transparent nor accountable. According to *The Economist*, "[t]he world is experiencing one of the biggest revolutions in history, as economic power shifts from the developed world to China and other emerging giants. Thanks to *market reforms*, emerging economies are growing much faster than developed

---

[49] "State-owned enterprises: Stakes and mistakes, India's government is privatizing companies for the wrong reasons," *The Economist*, www.economist.com/node/14845283, November 12, 2009.

[50] "Dancing elephants: Is Indian capitalism becoming oligarchic?" *The Economist*, www.economist.com/node/18010749?story_id=18010749, January 27, 2011.

[51] Ian Bremmer, "The Long Shadow of the Visible Hand: Government-owned firms control most of the world's oil reserves. Why the power of the state is back." *The Wall Street Journal*, http://online.wsj.com/article/SB10001424052748704852004575258541875590852.html, May 22, 2010.

ones."[52] Precisely! The quote is accurate in that it attributes the rise of emerging economies to market reforms. Where the premise fails is the assumption that these reforms are permanent. They aren't. These reforms are only laws, and like any laws, they can be rewritten.

It is not only that state-owned companies form a large part of emerging market economies. The problem is that the share is growing, not shrinking. The difficult market reforms that resulted in so many privatizations in the 1990s in China, India, and Russia were achieved at great cost and suffering. They were undertaken basically because there were few alternatives. But the economies of the BRICs and other emerging markets have done very well in the first decade of the twenty-first century. Even the Great Recession (Lesser Depression?) of 2008 hardly slowed down their growth.

Sadly, the governments in many of these countries have drawn the wrong conclusions about the reason for their growth. Their politicians believe that it was government policies and government-owned enterprises that saved them from the recession. The market was, and is, the enemy of the state. The process of renationalization has been going on for years, but the recession is a convenient pretext to accelerate a process that had started much earlier. The process involved a major assault on markets through an insidious process of renationalization.

In the good old days, a government that wished to nationalize (or renationalize) a company simply did so by decree. The most recent example was when Bolivia's President Evo Morales chose May 1, 2006 to lead troops into his country's biggest natural-gas field and read out a decree that gave Bolivia control. The glitch was that the owner of the gas was not some evil multinational corporation, but the state of Brazil through its state-owned gas company, Petrobras.

But Bolivia is the exception. These days, governments understand that outright nationalization is bad for business, especially foreign investment. So they have developed more subtle methods. For example, the takeover of oil-company Yukos and the jailing of its owner, Mikhail Khodorkovsky, by the state resulted from a charge of tax evasion. It helped to increase the state's share of the Russian stock market capitalization from 24% in 2004 to 40% in 2007.[53]

---

[52] "Dizzy in Boomtown: The boom in emerging economies and their stock markets is not over yet. But some are likely to run out of breath sooner than others," *The Economist*, http://www.economist.com/node/10136509, November 15, 2007.

[53] Carsten Spranger, "State Owned Enterprises in Russia," www.oecd.org/dataoecd/23/31/42576825.pdf, October 27, 2008.

Back to the Good Old Days

The recession provided an excuse for governments in emerging markets to provide money and liquidity to favored state firms while strangling private and foreign firms. In Russia, the state-owned banks, Sberbank and VTB, received enough new capital to be able to capture more than 50% of Russia's retail and corporate banking market. According to a senior western banker in Moscow, "After big liquidity injections by the government into state banks, most Russian businessmen are now mainly financed by Russian state banks. They are now lending on terms which would not get past credit committees in western institutions, and the western banks are moving out."[54] If the money is not lent, it is used for acquisitions, such as the recent acquisitions of the Bank of Moscow and TransCreditBank by VTB.

Buying private competition with state money is also popular in China. In 2009, when private companies were reeling from the economic downturn, the provincial government of Shandong used its control of Shandong Iron and Steel Group, the world's ninth-largest steelmaker by capacity, to attempt a takeover of the largest non-state steel group, Rizhao Iron and Steel. Rizhao's owner, Du Shuanghua was not happy about the prospect.

To prevent the merger, he tried a very Chinese poison pill. He handed up to 30% of Rizhao's shares to Kai Yuan Holdings at a low valuation. This Hong Kong–listed company was controlled by close relatives of Hu Jintao, the Chinese president. It didn't work. Protecting Du would have been too politically risky for Hu; so thus, the merger went through.[55]

Renationalization is not necessarily a product of bureaucratic ambitions or greed. Often, political considerations are involved. Huang Guangyu, founder of Gome, an electronics retailer, was at one time China's richest man. Like Khodorkovsky, he was seen by China's leaders as a potential threat to their power, so he was arrested in 2008.

Regulations are also used. If there is overcapacity or competition, the Chinese government will shut down smaller private firms, often citing pollution control or environmental issues as a reason. For example, the *Wall Street Journal* recently reported that "[t]he 10 largest [state-owned] steel mills raised their combined contribution to the country's total steel output to

---

[54] Catherine Belton, "Russia's state banks tighten their grip," *Financial Times,* www.ft.com, March 23, 2011.

[55] Jamil Anderlini, "China's Shandong Steel closes in on Rizhao," *Financial Times,* www.ft.com, August 25, 2009.

48% last year from 45% in 2009, and a total of 179 million tons of obsolete steel and iron capacity [often private] was shut down."[56]

The Chinese sovereign wealth fund also played a part in the renationalization process known in Chinese as "guojinmintui," or "the state advances as the private sector recedes." State-owned banks have to raise capital to cover an ever increasing amount of bad loans caused by the real estate bubble. Therefore, the China Investment Corporation, one of the country's many sovereign-wealth funds, stepped in and purchased shares of Chinese banks.

Implications for Investors

For direct investors, state-owned companies are a major headache. The economic purpose of contracts and a predictable legal infrastructure is to lower risk. If you know that the terms of your contract will be honored or if you know that the regulations will be administered fairly, you have a better chance of predicting the future and lowering your risk. State-owned companies, by definition, are owned by the entity that makes the rules, and the government—any government—like anyone else, does not like to lose money. If a government feels it can protect its investment by changing the rules, it will.

For example, Chinese state-owned companies have had a string of commodities disasters. Three state-owned Chinese airlines, Air China, Shanghai Airlines, and China Eastern, all had book losses totaling 13.17 billion yuan ($1.94 billion) as of the end of January 2009 on aviation fuel hedging contracts. In 2008 alone, the following state-owned Chinese companies had major losses. COSCO, the country's largest shipping group, had freight rates hedging losses of nearly 4 billion yuan ($585 million). CITIC Pacific, a steel-to-property conglomerate, had losses of up to $2 billion from unauthorized bets on forex markets. China Railway Group, the country's largest railway and highway builder, reported a 1.9 billion yuan ($278 million) foreign exchange loss, and China Railway Construction Corporation had forex losses of 320 million yuan ($47 million).[57] And these are only the ones we know about.

---

[56] Chuin-Wei Yap, "China to Renew Bid to Curb Steel Industry's Sprawl," *The Wall Street Journal,* http://online.wsj.com/article/SB10001424052748704721104576107153904581860. html#articleTabs=article, January 27, 2011.

[57] Eadie Chen and Jonathan Leff, "China state-owned corporate derivatives debacles," *Reuters,* www.forbes.com/feeds/afx/2009/07/27/afx6701999.html, July 27, 2009.

What were the solutions to these debacles? Simple—in each case, China broke the contracts. After all, the losses were not the result of managerial incompetence that would have put ordinary companies out of business. According to Li Wei, vice-director of the State-owned Assets Supervision and Administration Commission (SASAC), which is charged with monitoring state-owned companies, the losses were the fault of Goldman Sachs, Morgan Stanley, Merrill Lynch, and Citigroup, who were "closely associated with the intentionally complex and highly leveraged products that were fraudulently peddled by international investment banks with evil intentions."[58]

So SASAC "was investigating a number of derivatives deals and would help companies find ways to 'minimize losses.' "[59] In other words, "Stiffing the foreigners in pursuit of domestic policy goals is a time-honored practice here," says Arthur Kroeber at Dragonomics, a research company in Beijing.

But this does not apply only to financial contracts. Let us say that you are a multinational retailer like Wal-Mart. You open a store with a local state-owned company as a partner. After making a substantial investment, the store opens. Since it is new and better equipped than the smaller local competitors, it is an enormous success. For a few years the profits go through the roof. But then things begin to change.

Your local partner, probably owned by the local government, opens a store across the way called Chinamart. Chinamart looks exactly like your store. This is not surprising, because the manager used to work for you and took all of your intellectual property with him when he changed jobs. Chinamart uses all of your suppliers but pays less, because when they purchase products, they are not subject to a local tax. So Chinamart's prices are better. Then an official from the All China Federation of Trade Unions shows up and insists that you have to have a union. The union gets organized and goes on strike against the evil foreign corporation. Chinamart does not have a union and does not have to pay the higher wages that you have to pay as a result of the strike. Then another local government official shows up to inform you that your parking lot is unsafe and will be closed on weekends. It is closed to your customers, but not to the customers of Chinamart. Finally, you are informed that you have to have a communist party committee as part of your management. Chinamart has such a committee, often staffed with the same people or their relatives. You pay the members of your

---

[58] Jamil Anderlini, "Chinese official accuses western banks over losses," *Financial Times*, www.ft.com, December 4, 2009.

[59] Sundeep Tucker and Robert Cookson, "China talks tough on foreign bank derivatives," *Financial Times*, www.ft.com, September 14, 2009.

committee, and any plans that you make might immediately be used by Chinamart. You could sue in the local courts, but the judge is the brother-in-law of your former manager and works for the local Communist Party cadre that owns Chinamart. In fact, this hypothetical situation is not far off the mark. "Provincial governments favor provincial retailers. The national government gives a helping hand to all Chinese chains. Foreigners are on their own. Call it the Great Wall against Walmart."[60]

Indirect investors should be especially wary of putting their money into any state-owned company. The reason is quite simple. State-owned enterprises don't make money. The reason has to do with the economic problem of agency. In game theory, the best move for an agent, like corporate management, is to cheat the principals, the owners, and the shareholders. In law and economics, there are five incentives and disincentives that require managers of private companies to make a profit, and none apply to state-owned enterprises. It is not only the minority investors who are cheated; the real owners, the citizens of the state, are the real victims.

Besides the agency issue, state-owned companies are operated for political purposes, not for profit. Large state-owned energy companies in China and India constantly lose money because the price of their product is controlled. The price is not determined by the market price. High gas prices will cause social unrest, which politicians would prefer to avoid at the company's expense.

Corporate governance, transparency, and concern for minority shareholders basically do not exist. The interests of the politicians who run the government are always primary. They also run the courts, so there are no checks on power.

But the real reason why these companies should be avoided has to do with the reason why emerging markets have been attractive over the past decade. Market reforms in emerging markets have given a boost to their economies. Yet now, inefficient state-owned firms, which gorged themselves on taxpayer dollars, hidden taxes, subsidies, and regulatory preference, are coming back and, with them, the inefficiencies that plagued these economies. When these things were pared down thanks to reform, these economies became more efficient and were able to obtain better growth. But now that they are back, these economies will become less efficient and growth will slow. Market reforms do not last forever.

---

[60] "Retailing in China: Walmart v Wumart," *The Economist*, www.economist.com/blogs/schumpeter/2011/05/retailing_china, May 18, 2011.

Lack of Information

Relationship-based systems are not a way station on the road to rule-based systems. On the contrary, once in existence, it is very hard to create an economically efficient legal framework. The reason is simple economics. A relationship-based system is too profitable for those in charge to create something else.

Relationship-based Economies Thrive on Connections and Information

Every aspect of a relationship-based system tends to support the other parts. Large family-run firms use their connections and bribes to win contracts from state-run firms. State-run firms provide money and patronage for the party in power. The artificial competitive advantages enjoyed by family- and state-owned firms force smaller, more efficient private firms into the underground economy. The cycle is endlessly repeated throughout emerging markets.

State-owned banks help this process by showering money on state-owned firms in times of economic stress to create jobs in case of social unrest. In Egypt, the Mubarak regime used jobs as well as subsidies to hang onto power. Between Egypt's state-owned companies and a huge civil service that employs 7 million people, the state provides jobs for over one-third of the workforce, three times the number in OECD countries.[61]

State-owned banks only lend to those firms that provide the best credit risk, a small club that includes only other state-owned and favored family firms. Often, the banks are well capitalized and have large portions of their assets invested in local government bonds, which support local bureaucrats. All while the most productive part of the economy, the small- to medium-size businesses, goes without.

A large, useless set of regulations cannot be removed because it favors rent-seeking bureaucrats. It also limits competition with inefficient state-owned and large family businesses. The overlay of regulations governed by corrupt officials makes it almost impossible to do business. To facilitate income-tax refunds in India, "where the standard 'charge' is 10%," says *The Economist*,

---

[61] "How to stay in charge. Not just coercion, sham democracy too," *The Economist*, www.economist.com/node/14027720, July 23, 2009.

"sums between 5,000 and 50,000 rupees change hands."[62] With oppressive regulations, the only alternative for a small private business to survive is to operate in a grey or black economy.

Operating below the radar may work, but it limits the size of businesses. Businesses cannot expand and take advantage of economies of scale because they cannot get capital from state-owned banks, nor do they have the connections or funds to bribe the right official to grant a permit or ignore an absurd regulation.

Investors Beware

Relationship-based systems also make it very difficult for foreign investors. Small changes and reforms within these economies can often bring dramatic results. But just because people are making money in emerging markets does not mean that a foreign investor will profit. In order to make money, there has to be some sort of nexus between the investment and the enterprise. Agreements to manage for the benefit of shareholders, pay money back, or perform contracts have to be honored and enforced by competent courts. Advantages that make foreign investment attractive to the locals and give them incentives to comply might be short-lived. If circumstances change, investors may find that their lucrative enterprise is based on nothing more than worthless paper.

This tends to make the investment cycle short and volatile. Investors can only invest based on conditions as they exist in the present. When anything changes, it is time to leave. For example, you can do business by bribing an official, but bribing the right official with the right amount is difficult. If the official changes jobs, is purged or even arrested, then the deal is off. This is why the concept of "guanxi," which is often translated as connections or relationships, is so important in China. This is why Dhirubhai Ambani cultivated everyone from the doorman on up.

Accurate Public Information: A Rare Commodity

But the worst victim of these systems is information. Investors flatter themselves in this world of computers, social networking, the Internet, and 24-hour global news that information is accurate, complete, and timely. Nothing could be further from the truth.

---

[62] "India's chief economic adviser wants to legalise some kinds of bribe-giving," *The Economist*, www.economist.com/node/18652037, May 5, 2011.

Information has enormous value. It is not just given away. It is traded only for an economic incentive, consideration, or a legal disincentive. For example, in the United States, certain information is required to be disclosed by securities laws. As the recent case of hedge fund manager Raj Rajaratnam proved, Mr. Rajaratnam was making money because he was trading on "insider information," which basically means that he knew things the rest of the market didn't. The information he illegally purchased cost him a great deal. The violation of US securities laws will cost him more. He faces up to 20 years in prison.

Relationship-based systems have no such disincentives. The Chinese spend more on their internal security than their armed forces,[63] but the watchdogs are basically impotent, because they can't really police themselves. The Chinese version of the SEC, the China Securities Regulatory Commission (CSRC), is supposed to prevent fraud, but it is supervising mostly, perhaps exclusively, state-owned corporations that all have protectors within the government. With such an enormous conflict of interest, it is doubtful that it provides any disincentive at all.

Corruption is, by definition, something that is illegal. Why would any party to a corrupt transaction reveal any information about it? For both sides to the transaction, it can be exceptionally lucrative. The person paying the bribe or making the connection has an enormous competitive advantage over any other player. The person receiving the bribe is simply selling information and has no reason to stop.

Family-owned firms have enormous economic incentives to protect their interests in their companies. In countries where corporate governance is lacking, they have few, if any, legal disincentives to actually disclose information; often they don't. The interests of the family will always come before the interests of the minority shareholders.

Investors looking for accurate information often rely on the work of multinational accounting firms. But these firms are not unified. Instead, they are networks of independent firms stitched together to form an international entity. As such, local firms are still subject to local pressures. For example, when Grant Thornton's Hong Kong affiliate was to be integrated with Grant Thornton's mainland affiliate, a company named Jingdu Tianhua, more than 600 accountants from the Hong Kong office left en masse. The circumstance of their departure depends on whether you believe Grant Thornton, who

---

[63] Leslie Hook, "Beijing raises spending on internal security," *Financial Times*, www.ft.com, March 6, 2011.

said the ex-employees were expelled, or the ex-employees, who insisted that they resigned. In either case, all the ex-employees were immediately hired by Hong Kong competitor BDO.[64]

The action by the entire staff of one of the world's largest accounting firms does give an indication of the difference in standards between Hong Kong firms and mainland Chinese firms. Patrick Rozario, the chief executive who led the exodus, would only say that BDO's independence was a "model that suits us better."[65] However, wrote *The Economist*, "at least one big investment bank is said to be reluctant to use any accountancy outfit other than the Hong Kong offices of the big four for public offerings, because of concerns about the quality of the work."[66]

In India in 2009, the Indian market collapsed 13% in one week in dollar terms. The cause, according to the *Financial Times*, was because "investor confidence in the quality of corporate information on the subcontinent has collapsed in the wake of the accounting fraud at Satyam. Satyam was fourth-largest of India's legendary outsourcing IT services firm."[67] It was also family owned. The fantastic growth of corporate profits, almost six-fold between 2003 and 2008, was now in question. The firm's auditor was PwC, the largest accounting firm in the world. Two of its auditors were arrested by the Indian police.[68] Recently, an Indian research firm, Ambit Research, published a study stating that, over the past four years, the accounting quality in India has deteriorated, most often in large-cap companies.[69]

All markets are dependent upon accurate information about the state of the economy. Often, this information is distorted by government action. For example, the Baltic Dry Index (BDI) is a measure of freight rates for shipping iron ore, coal, and grain. As the demand for these commodities increases with economic activity, the rates rise, given the limited amount of ships available. For much of its 26-year history, the BDI has accurately been described

[64] "Hard numbers: Betrayal, loss and new love among auditors," *The Economist*, www.economist.com/node/17633120, December 2, 2010.

[65] Enoch Yiu, "Troubled accounting firm's staff jump ship," *South China Morning Post*, http://archive.scmp.com, November 3, 2010.

[66] "Hard numbers: Betrayal, loss and new love among auditors," *The Economist*, www.economist.com/node/17633120, December 2, 2010.

[67] Lex, "Indian corporate governance," *Financial Times*, www.ft.com, January 12, 2009.

[68] Joe Leahy, "PwC staff detained in Satyam probe," *Financial Times*, www.ft.com, January 25, 2009.

[69] Munira Dongre, "Ambit uneasy over deterioration of accounting quality," *MoneyLife*, www.moneylife.in/article/81/11919.html, December 6, 2010.

as "the supreme cyclical indicator."[70] It has closely tracked the price of commodities and the ebb and flow of economic activity. However, with the rise of China and state-dominated demand, its predictive value has decreased. It has been yo-yoing since 2002, when the demand from China started to go into high gear.[71]

In the last year, the index has seemingly gone haywire. Capesize vessels, huge 1,000-foot ships that are too large to go through the Suez and Panama canals, used to rent for more than the smaller Panamax. But since July 2009, they have been launched from shipyards at a rate of 15 per month, increasing the capacity of the global fleet at an average annual rate of 20%. Although 3.7% of the current fleet will be demolished this year, a record proportion, the Chinese state-controlled and -subsidized shipyards have increased new capacity by 15%. What is the reason for this? The Chinese government wants cheap freight to help subsidize their growing demand for commodities and the output of their manufacturing. So they are willing to operate their construction and shipping sectors at a loss. The result of this subsidy, besides bankruptcies for other shipping firms, is the distortion of the index beyond all relation to the real state of the global economy.

China is also suffering a shortage of electricity. Some economists might conclude that this has to do with vibrant economic growth, but it is really about misguided subsidies. Chinese electric companies are state-controlled, as are the electricity prices. China is facing an enormous problem with inflation, the result of massive state-mandated bank loans flooding the economy with money. The companies are facing financial pressure as global energy costs increase. But Beijing keeps prices low to control inflation.

To avoid losses, the companies tell the authorities that they will produce electricity at full capacity, but privately, they cut back supply. Without reliable power, manufacturers and businesses use diesel generators for electricity. This, of course, increases the demand and the price for diesel and helps to fuel inflation. It also confuses the economic signals upon which businesses and investors depend.

---

[70] Gwen Robinson, "Why the Baltic Dry Index Matters," http://ftalphaville.ft.com/blog/2008/01/30/10578/why-the-baltic-dry-index-matters/, January 30, 2008.

[71] Lex, "Shipping costs," *Financial Times*, September 28, 2008.

Free Speech: Don't Take it for Granted

The largest impediment to accurate timely and complete information in emerging markets is free speech. Free speech is usually considered a political luxury, something to indulge the chattering classes, rather than a crucial element for successful businesses and growth. This is false. It is not only an admirable human right, but the most effective protection for investors. More than any other element for long-term investing, free speech is vital and irreplaceable.

The contradiction to this thesis is, of course, China. Since the Chinese Communist Party took over China in 1949, speech has been severely restricted. It is not just public demonstrations, like those suppressed in Tiananmen Square in 1989, the constant demonstrations against tainted products, or the uncompensated confiscation of farm land for rampant development; it is basically everything that could reflect poorly on either the state or its rulers.

Without free speech and a free press, there is no one to question or investigate anything. There is no disincentive by government bureaucrats or corporate officers to ever reveal the truth about any aspect of China's economic reality. Without precise information, the market does not have the economic signals necessary to achieve its true function, which is the efficient allocation of capital.

It is not only foreign direct or indirect investors who can be harmed by this lack of information, but also the government itself. Every policy decision made in China is based on incorrect information.

Turn on any news program in the United States. There is always an intense debate as to who is telling the truth. This debate goes on not only on television, but also on the radio, the Internet, and in newspapers and magazines, 24/7. Corporate offices, universities and colleges, and government agencies are all involved. Investigative reporters have large economic incentives to ferret out the truth. This provides tension with businesses and politicians who have large economic incentives to distort it. Americans produce terabytes of all sorts of silliness from pages of useless statistics to tweets of idle gossip. But in this enormous pile of information, there is truth.

As John Maynard Keynes remarked, "When the facts change, I change my mind. What do you do, sir?"[72] Without free and open uninhibited debate, investigation, questions, and argument, the facts are never revealed. No

---

[72] Alfred L. Malabre, Jr., *Lost Prophets: An Insider's History of the Modern Economists* (Cambridge Massachusetts: Harvard Business Press, 1994), p. 220.

bureaucrats or corporate executives interested in keeping their jobs or qualifying for promotion would ever think of providing bad news about a failed policy unless there was absolutely no way to hide it.

In China, all of the incentives are to portray both the country and the party in the best light possible. The Communist Party's rule has not lasted 60 years because they highlighted their failures. China would never have been able to attract billions of foreign direct investment if its publicity machine had not worked overtime. Even China's in-house advertising agency's name is telling. In English, it is known as the Publicity Department of the Communist Party of China. Its name in Chinese reveals its real purpose. It is still known as the Propaganda Department.[73]

The maxim of successful propaganda and advertising is to state your presumption loud enough and often enough until people assume that it is true. In China and any other country that suppresses information, truth will lose all meaning. But this is not just for the citizens of a particular country who may not have the benefit of other sources of information. In prior years, the Chinese economy was a rounding error for the global economy. Since this is no longer true, distortions that are created in China do not stay in China. It is not only the Chinese markets that do not receive the proper signals, but the rest of the world as well.

Propaganda tends to fill gaps when accurate information is not available. It can happen even in the United States. For example, WorldCom's executive, John Sidgmore, repeated claims in the late 1990s that the company's Internet traffic was doubling every 90 days—an effective 800% annual growth rate. It was accepted carte blanche by government, industry, and the media. Indeed, the chief of the US FCC at the time, Reed Hundt, regularly parroted the number.[74] The result was an economic and financial disaster, and this was in the United States, where free press and free speech are sacrosanct. What is going on in China is anyone's guess. Yet billions are invested daily, based on nothing more than claims and information repeated so often that it has achieved the status of truth.

China is an extreme example of the suppression of free speech. In other emerging markets, the distortion of information is not so blatant. In Russia,

---

[73] Zhang, Xiaoling; Zheng, Yongnian, *China's Information and Communications Technology Revolution: Social Changes and State Responses.* Taylor & Francis. p. 104. "The English translation has been changed to 'Publicity Department' but the Chinese term remains 'Propaganda Department'," 2009.

[74] Yochi J. Dreazen, "Wildly Optimistic Data Drove Telecoms to Build Fiber Glut," *Wall Street Journal*, www.onlineWSJ.com, September, 2002.

information is not explicitly suppressed, but journalists are routinely intimidated, bribed, or simply killed. Often the distortion of information is simply the result of incompetence. Statisticians are often underfunded and their ability to gather accurate data is quite limited.

Implications for Investors

The end lesson for both direct and indirect investors is that the combination of family corporations, large underground economies, corruption, state-owned firms, and restrictions on freedom of the press and speech result in the simple fact that the stream of information produced by all emerging markets is not accurate, is never complete, and is often months out of date.

The utilization of modern financial and economic tools that were developed and refined for sophisticated developed markets with accurate, complete, and timely information should be used with great care in emerging markets, if at all. Explanations by economists that involve acrobatic reasoning to force emerging market economies into the theoretical molds of the developed market should be avoided.

To circumnavigate these issues, investors, where possible, should rely on information that they or an independent firm develops. If data is provided, its provenance should be clearly stated. Careful investors should know exactly to what extent information is derived from government sources and whether those sources have any credibility. In recent years, many private firms have sprung up, even in China. These local companies understand the local problems and give a far more accurate picture than international news sources, no matter how good these sources are.

Investors should consider what the incentives and disincentives are for the source. In September of 2007, I gave a speech in front of the Vancouver CFA society, predicting that the Chinese stock market was a bubble and would soon rapidly deflate. I was challenged by a member of the audience who pointed out that my thesis was contrary to predictions of at least one major Wall Street investment bank. I countered that their incentive was to sell product, while mine was far more benign. I don't think the questioner was convinced, but the market topped out two months later and soon lost over 70% of its value.

If you want to avoid such losses, investors should understand that relationship-based systems do work differently. If you can understand exactly how and why, you will have a chance to separate the hype from the reality and actually make some money in these markets or at least avoid losing it.

China

The People's Republic of China has enjoyed spectacular growth for much of the past twenty years. Annual growth rates in double digits are quite common and nearly the expected norm. Although China's growth rate slowed for a few quarters, the Great Recession scarcely influenced it, and it soon powered back to reestablish breathtaking growth.

This year, China surpassed Japan to become the world's second largest economy. Seldom does a day go by without a prediction of its coming dominance of the world's economy. Experts from around the world, at every level, from consulting firms to government agencies, are all competing to predict the continuation of China's rise. All manner of financial advisors, from television personalities to amateurs, incessantly promulgate the thesis that rapid growth of the Chinese economy is inevitable and any alternative analysis is absurd. At the time of this writing, the most recent analysis was from the accounting firm PricewaterhouseCoopers (PwC), which stated that "China could overtake the United States to become the world's largest banking economy by 2023."[1]

A continuing element of this hypothesis is the shift of power from West to East. The PwC report repeats this dogma: "The shift of financial power was accelerated by the financial crisis, from which banks in emerging markets escaped relatively unscathed. China's rise to become the world's leading

---

[1] Chris Oliver, "China to Emerge Global Banking Leader by 2023: PWC," *MarketWatch*, June 3, 2011, http://www.marketwatch.com/story/china-to-emerge-global-banking-leader-by-2023-pwc-2011-06-03.

banking economy is coming along 20 years earlier than had been forecast prior to the financial crisis."[2] Continuously repeated until the assumption attained the level of a basic truth, that reality alone should be enough to put investors on their guard. China certainly warrants caution.

It is impossible to argue that China has not grown. It is impossible to argue that China's growth has not been spectacular. It is impossible to argue that China's growth has not pulled millions of people out of poverty. Nonetheless, projecting that the present trend will continue indefinitely into the future is not realistic. At some point, every economic forecast will be wrong.

The next assumption can be even more disastrous for investors. A growing economy means that someone is getting rich. This does not mean that everyone, especially foreign investors, will necessarily share in that bounty. No matter how sophisticated, no matter how well connected, without the protection of a good legal infrastructure, foreign investors are vulnerable to deception, both directly and indirectly.

Paulson & Co. is a hedge fund run by the legendary investor and billionaire John Paulson. Paulson is one of the savviest and best-informed investors on Wall Street. His company has $37 billion under its management. His fund made $4 billion betting against subprime mortgages.[3] The result of some of his bets helped the demise of Lehman Brothers. After Lehman fell, he began purchasing its bonds for a fraction of their value and now might make a 78% profit on the transaction.[4]

But for all of Paulson's expertise, he is helpless in China. His hedge fund made an investment in a Chinese forestry company called Sino-Forest. Indeed, his fund owns 14.13% of Sino-Forest's outstanding shares and it was the largest shareholder. However, Paulson is not the only shareholder. According to the *Financial Times*, Sino-Forest shares are also owned by other large fund managers, including Hartford Investment Management (3.2%), Blackrock, Vanguard, and Henderson Global.[5]

---

[2] Ibid.

[3] Matt Wirz, Mike Spector, and Tom Mcginty, "Paulson Plays the Lehman Bust: Hedge Fund Poised to Score Big on Doomed Bank's Bonds; a 78% Return?" *Wall Street Journal*, May 10, 2011, http://online.wsj.com/article/SB100014240527487046819045763132209 63273398.html?KEYWORDS=Paulson++co.

[4] Ibid.

[5] Stacy-Marie Ishmael and John McDermott, "A $4.2bn question for Sino-Forest Corporation," *Financial Times, FT Tilt, FT Alphaville,* June 2, 2011, http://www.ft.com.

Paulson & Co.'s investment was worth US$646 million. Not anymore. From April to June of 2011, the stock, listed on the Toronto Stock Exchange, dropped over 92%. The reason? A report by the Canadian research firm, Muddy Waters, caused the stock to fall.[6]

Muddy Waters alleged, among other things, that "the $231.1 million in Yunnan province timber [that Sino-Forest] claimed to sell is largely fabricated." Why? Because, "Transporting the harvested logs would have required over 50,000 trucks driving on two-lane roads winding through the mountains from this remote region, which is far beyond belief [and likely road capacity]."[7] It also pointed out that Sino-Forest overstated its purchases by over $800 million and its corporate structure utilized over 20 British Virgin Island entities.

Paulson liquidated his position in Sino-Forest for a loss of $500 million.[8]

Paulson & Co. is not the only such example. With $106 billion of capital under its management, the Carlyle Group is one of the largest and most famous of the private equity firms. Known for its ability to attract the best-connected people in the world, including former US President George H. W. Bush and James Baker, III, a former United States Secretary of State, it has employed heads of the United Kingdom, Thailand, and the Philippines, and legions of former ministers from various countries. The Carlyle Group has even been the subject of a Michael Moore movie, *Fahrenheit 911*.[9]

Carlyle is one of the most successful private equity groups in China. Some of its investments have, at least on paper, generated excellent returns for its grateful investors. However, even Carlyle has problems. China Forestry, a Chinese lumber products firm (similar to Sino-Forest), received an investment of about $55 million from Carlyle before it went through its Hong Kong initial public offering (IPO) in December 2009. By May 2011, it posted a $417 million annual loss and its auditor, KPMG, stated that it could not vouch for the accuracy of the group's financial results because of incomplete books and records. To compound the matter, its CEO, Li Han Chun, found himself arrested in China—for allegedly embezzling $4.6 million.[10]

---

[6] Dan McCrum and Robert Cookson, "Plunge Triggers Trading Halt for China Forestry Group," *Financial Times*, June 3, 2011, http://www.ft.com.

[7] Ibid.

[8] Dan McCrum, "Paulson Fund Loses $500m on Sino Stake," *Financial Times*, June 21, 2011, http://www.ft.com.

[9] "Carlyle Group," Wikipedia, May 29, 2011, http://en.wikipedia.org/wiki/Carlyle_Group.

[10] Robert Cookson and Henny Sender, "Carlyle Faces Questions Over China Investments," *Financial Times*, May 5, 2011, http://www.ft.com.

China Forestry was not the only dud investment by Carlyle in China. China Agritech is a NASDAQ–listed fertilizer maker in which Carlyle has a 22% stake. At $31.21 a share, its shares reached an all-time high on February 1, 2010. It is now trading at $2.81 a share—a fall of 91%. In 2011, it was suspended from trading and is now fighting delisting for failure to file its accounts in a timely manner.[11]

David Rubenstein, the co-founder of Carlyle, defended its investments in China and claimed that most of the 50 deals it had done in China were, at least on paper, profitable. Others weren't so confident. According to an executive at another big international private equity group, "To have two go wrong in such quick succession is somewhere between careless and unlucky."[12]

It wasn't just the investments of Paulson and Carlyle that went bad. In the first six months of 2011, the *Financial Times* reported that "25 New York-listed Chinese companies have disclosed accounting discrepancies or seen their auditors resign."[13] In May 2011, the NASDAQ suspended 19 stocks from trading. Fifteen of those were Chinese.[14]

Many of the companies listed in the US that are having problems, like Sino-Forest, went public in so-called "reverse mergers." American securities law, in a normal IPO, requires a company to issue a lengthy prospectus, which has to provide certified accounts for several years. Conversely, in a "back door registration"—a reverse merger—the company purchases a shell of a listed company and then merges into that company. (A shell is a public corporation, stripped of its assets, which has outlived its original purpose.) Going public with an IPO can be very expensive, and the reverse merger is a far cheaper way to raise capital on US public markets without many of the costs. In addition, it allows companies to avoid some of the disclosure and the vetting by regulators, investors, and underwriters.

Reverse mergers have been particularly attractive to Chinese companies. Since 2007, there have been 600 reverse mergers. A quarter of them have been Chinese.[15] Over the past few years, many of these stocks have done

---

[11] Ibid.

[12] Ibid.

[13] Robert Cookson, "China Foreign Listings Dogged by Scandal," *Financial Times*, June 5, 2011, http://www.ft.com.

[14] Robert Cookson and Henny Sender, "Carlyle faced questions over their investments in China." *Financial Times*, May 5, 2011, www.ft.com.

[15] "Reversal of Fortune: Beware of Chinese Bus–Advertising Firms Backing into Shell Companies," *The Economist*. http://www.economist.com/node/18530335, April 7, 2011.

quite well. With the craze for Chinese stocks, almost any company with Sino or China in its name jumped, sometimes with spectacular results. China Agritech rose over 1000% from 2007 to its height in 2010. The China "story" and the unending growth of China and all things relating to China seemed like a sure bet, and investors weren't particular about how the companies came to market.

Now, the trends have unquestionably reversed. Any Chinese stock that came to the market in a reverse merger is currently under severe short-selling pressure. (In "shorting" shares, investors are betting that the price of a stock will go down.) In fact, there were so many problems with Chinese shares, by the end of June 2011, another shortage appeared. According to Jim Chanos, who is the most prominent of the China bears, "It was getting hard to find such shares to short, so big are the positions already against them."[16]

Nonetheless, it wasn't just the stocks of new small companies; bonds of well-known, seemingly reputable, established companies in China can be parsimonious with information. Established in 1995, Nine Dragons is well established and one of the world's largest paperboard producers. Its chief executive and largest shareholder is Zhang Yin. She ranked number one in the 2010 rankings of China's richest women and has a personal fortune of $5.6 billion. Nine Dragons has $50 million of bonds outstanding, with the bulk owned by state-owned banks.[17] "S&P said it had withdrawn its BB long-term corporate rating on Nine Dragons because it had been given 'insufficient access' to management in the past six months although it had repeatedly requested meetings."[18]

Nonetheless, the foolishness continues. Yongye International is a NASDAQ-listed Chinese fertilizer producer. With food prices at record highs and China's growth a universal given, it seemed like a sure bet. But, in May 2011, it fell 20% after accusations of fraud by a Wyoming-based hedge fund, Absaroka Capital Management. Fortunately, Yongye had a savior. A private equity arm of Morgan Stanley invested $50 million into the company and stated that Yongye was "an exceptional company." With Wall Street's stamp of approval, which apparently trumps Wyoming's invectives, Yongye's shares bounced back 40%.[19]

---

[16] Simon Rabinovitch, "Is China Bubble Now an Anti–China Bubble?," *Financial Times*, June 3, 2011, http://www.ft.com.

[17] Robert Cookson, "S&P Withdraws Nine Dragons Paper Rating," *Financial Times*, June 3, 2011, http://www.ft.com.

[18] Ibid.

[19] Robert Cookson, "China Foreign Listings Dogged by Scandal," *Financial Times*, June 5, 2011, http://www.ft.com.

So, what exactly is the quandary? What are firms like Paulson, Carlyle, perhaps Morgan Stanley, and many other economists and financial analysts failing to see? Quite simply, they live in a world of numbers. Like most of the sophisticated clients of Bernie Madoff, the consideration of fabricated numbers at that level would not occur to them. Neither would it occur to them that the numbers reported in China are merely a guide and not necessarily the truth. The really sad part is that it isn't like the Chinese haven't warned them.

One Billion Capitalists

In my research, I came across the following quotation: "The world is experiencing one of the biggest revolutions in history, as economic power shifts from the developed world to China and other emerging giants. Thanks to *market reforms*, emerging economies are growing much faster than developed ones [emphasis added]."[20] Written for *The Economist* in 2007, the sentiment is quite familiar. You hear it often, usually as part of the phrase "the story is quite compelling." The quote is accurate in that it attributes the rise of emerging economies to market reforms. Where the premise fails is in the assumption that these reforms are permanent. They aren't. These reforms are only laws. Laws are mere pieces of paper. Like any law, they can be rewritten. This is especially true of China.

The financial world seems intent on treating China like a market economy. It isn't. It is still a command economy, as the European Union has often stated.[21] One would think that people would notice that China's flag is modeled after the flag of the old Soviet Union, the name of the country is the People's Republic, and that it is run by a political party that proudly calls itself the Communist Party. Despite the hype, the Chinese economy is very much dominated by the state and it intends to stay that way.

In his excellent book, *Capitalism with Chinese Characteristics,*[22] MIT Professor Yasheng Huang repeatedly points out why this is true with China. Examined in contrast to India, the Indian economy is supposedly still subject to the legacy of socialism. Yet, according to Professor Huang, at the height of Indian

---

[20] "The boom in emerging economies and their stock markets is not over yet. But some are likely to run out of breath sooner than others." *The Economist,* November 15, 2007, http://www.economist.com/node/10136509.

[21] Victor Mallet, "Beijing Pursues European Charm Offensive," *Financial Times,* January 5, 2011, http://www.ft.com.

[22] Yasheng Huang, *Capitalism with Chinese Characteristics: Entrepreneurship and the State,* Cambridge University Press, New York, 2008.

socialism in the 1980s, the private share of fixed asset investment was 58%. In China, as recently as 2005, it was only 33.5%.[23] Even worse, according to Professor Huang, "We now have convincing evidence that productivity growth has slowed substantially since the late 1990s. The slowdown in productivity means the current rapid GDP growth rates are not sustainable."[24]

But the Chinese leadership has no interest in reining in the government. On the contrary, China and its new leaders are sparking a "red revival," with definite throwbacks to the Cultural Revolution. In Chongqing, a rising star of the younger Communist leadership, Bo Xilai, a princeling as the son of Bo Yibo, one of China's "eight immortals,"[25] is encouraging Maoist slogans and propaganda techniques. There was a giant bronze statue of Confucius in Tiananmen Square; but, in April of 2011, it suddenly disappeared. Confucius was a prime target for the violent Red Guards and a powerful symbol of a changed China. Although both he and his father, a revolutionary guerilla leader, suffered under the Cultural Revolution, the man slated to be the next leader of China, Xi Jinping, had been described "as being redder than red."[26]

The return of Maoist-era rhetoric is supposed to be evidence of the Chinese government's crackdown on society to prevent a Chinese version of the Arab Spring. However, there is also a strong economic element. For years, the Chinese government has been slowly renationalizing parts of its economy. In the past, governments would routinely take over private businesses. That is not so today. Now, they use far subtler means. They buy them.

In Chapter 2, we saw the provincial government of Shandong purchase the private company Rizhao. In December 2010, the provincial government of China's biggest steelmaking province, Hebei, bought 10% of seven private steel mills for its Hebei Iron and Steel Company. This was in addition to the 10% of another five steel firms that the state-owned company bought a month earlier.[27]

---

[23] Ibid., 278.

[24] Ibid., 288.

[25] John Garnaut, "Children of the Revolution," *Sydney Morning Herald*, February 10, 2010, http://www.smh.com.au/world/children-of-the-revolution-20100212-nxjh.html.

[26] Geoff Dyer, "Who Will be China's Next Leaders?," *Financial Times*, March 4, 2011, http://www.ft.com.

[27] Michael Sainsbury, "China Privatisation Machine into Reverse," *The Australian*, January 27, 2011, http://www.theaustralian.com.au/business/china-privatisation-machine-into-reverse/story-e6frg8zx-1225995084947.

Other methods of renationalization include arresting the principal, not for political considerations, such as with Huang Guangyu, the founder of Gome electronics, but for simple greed. Managers of a state-owned travel business in Guangzhou sold out to an Australian businessman named Mr. Ng. When Mr. Ng turned the business into a successful money machine and the value of its assets had multiplied, another state-owned company, Guangzhou Lingnan, decided that the sale was a mistake. They arranged to have Mr. Ng arrested for bribery and embezzlement and then they confiscated the company. Despite the personal promise by none other than Premier Wen Jiabao to Australian Prime Minister Julia Gillard that Mr. Ng would receive an open trial, agents and employees of Guangzhou Lingnan packed the courtroom. When questioned by foreign Australian journalists, the Lingnan official refused to answer questions, arguing in Chinese that he could not speak Chinese.[28]

The Chinese sovereign wealth fund also played a part in the renationalization process known in Chinese as "guojinmintui," or "the state advances as the private sector recedes." State-owned banks have to raise capital to cover an ever-increasing amount of bad loans caused by the real estate bubble. To cover the bad loans and replace lost capital, in steps, the China Investment Corporation (CIC), one of the country's many sovereign-wealth funds, purchases shares of Chinese banks.[29] Basically, this process is a state bailout of the banking system by another name.

Crumbling Financial System

The CIC was buying shares in the Chinese banks because they needed to. Rather than stimulating the economy through direct government-financed packages, the Chinese have been stimulating their economy with loans from the state banks. Chinese banks are flush with money gained through a sophisticated system of financial repression.

Financial repression is a process where the government—through regulations, capital controls, and reserve requirements—limits the investment alternatives for investors and savers. It allows governments to channel investments to political priorities at below-market rates. In the West after World War II, it allowed governments to quickly pay off the mountain of debt incurred during the war. Japan's system was particularly sophisticated

---

[28] "China's Justice System Exposed," *Brisbane Times*, August 11, 2011, www.brisbanetimes.com.au/opinion/editorial/chinas-justice-system-exposed-20110810-1impp.html#ixzz1UjQNCUob.

[29] "So Much for Capitalism: The Opening up of China's Economy Goes into Reverse," *The Economist*, March 5, 2009, www.economist.com/node/13235115.

since it extended to specific tax incentives and disincentives. In most developed countries today, the free flow of capital allows not only different types of investments, but also investments in different countries. So, financial repression is no longer possible. But not in China.

The Chinese have successfully walled off their financial system from the rest of the world and their currency is not convertible. Seen as a virtue during the Asian crisis of 1997 and the 2008 financial crisis, China was effectively quarantined from the global financial infections. However, this does not prevent homegrown illnesses. China has a massive bad loan problem and it is getting worse.

The problem has three interconnecting sources. First, as a relationship-based system, the state banks lend to other state institutions, such as state-owned firms and local governments. Small- to medium-sized private companies, especially those without party connections, are either starved of capital or borrow in the grey market. Second, as I wrote in 2004,[30] in China, it is very difficult to collect a debt. When the state bank lends to another state entity, the failure to pay back a loan is almost looked upon as a wash. Except in rare instances, formal bankruptcies do not occur. The result is that bad loans are basically either never collected or written off. Finally, the lack of a functioning tax system, especially a real property tax, makes local governments reliant on land sales financed by cheap loans that support a real estate bubble.

The bad debt problem has been around since the last recession in 1999. At that time, the four largest state banks moved approximately $250 billion worth of bad loans into corresponding "bad banks," called asset management companies (AMC). This was in exchange for bonds, which were worth the face value of the bad debts. The AMCs where supposed to sell or dispose of the debts for the best price possible and wind down in a decade. The problem was that the best price was often only a few cents on the dollar.

If the size of the debts became known, it might have threatened the financial system and could have been particularly embarrassing during the 2005 IPOs of Bank of China, Industrial and Commercial Bank of China (ICBC), and China Construction Bank. So, after 10 years, when it came time for the AMCs to disappear, their tenure was simply extended and the bonds, which make up part of the capital of the banks, were simply rolled over.[31]

---

[30] William Gamble, "Going Bust: Overcoming a Dysfunctional Credit System," *Harvard International Review*, May 6, 2006, http://hir.harvard.edu/china/going-bust.

[31] Heard on the Street, "The Chinese 10–Year Plan for Bad Debt," *Wall Street Journal*, September 23, 2009, http://www.wsj.com.

The bad debt problem did not go away after the 1999 recession. In 2006, UBS estimated that the non-performing loans of the big four and other Chinese banks was only around 30%.[32] It only got "better" at the time three of the big four listed in IPOs and the problem was pronounced cured. But it wasn't.

Local governments do not have the power to levy real estate taxes on any residential property. So, their major source of revenue is through land sales. Since land in China is not owned but leased from the government on long-term leases, local governments have the power to remove its citizens from valuable property and "sell" it to developers. To make this system work requires loans from state-owned banks to developers, who "buy" the land. It also requires constantly rising real estate prices. We looked at some of the results of this program in Chapter 1, when we discussed the empty town of Chenggong.

As a case in point, in 2009, land sales by China's local governments generated 1.6 trillion yuan (around $233 billion); this represents a 60% increase from a year earlier and at least half of the local governments' fiscal revenue.[33] As land prices go up, so does local government revenue. So, both the developers and the local government have enormous interests in keeping property prices rising. The fuel for this Ponzi scheme is loans from the state-owned, but often locally controlled, banks. If real estate prices decline, the whole system goes with it.

Of course, after the crash, the Chinese government relied on its banks to stimulate the economy, and stimulate they did. It became a competition. For example, a provincial governor confided in a Chinese economist that his greatest political achievement for 2009 was that bank lending in his province had outpaced the national average.[34] In 2009 alone, they lent a record 9.6 trillion yuan ($1.4 trillion). If the US stimulus had been on a similar size relative to GDP, it would have been $6 trillion. The lending in 2010 was on a similar scale, 7.95 trillion yuan (about $1.2 trillion USD).[35] In contrast, in 2008, there were only 4 trillion yuan ($585 billion USD) in new loans.

---

[32] "Keep Growing," *The Economist*, March 23, 2006, http://www.economist.com/node/5623341.

[33] Craig Stephen, "China Government Finances Exposed to Land Bubble: Commentary: Mainland Follows Hong Kong's High–Risk Revenue Model," *MarketWatch*, February 8, 2010, http://www.marketwatch.com/story/hong-kong-trades-its-way-to-budget-surplus-2010-02-08.

[34] Richard McGregor, "China's Banks Lend with Communist Zeal," *Financial Times*, July 8 2009, http://www.ft.com.

[35] "New Yuan Loans Hit 7.95 Trillion Yuan in 2010," *People's Daily Online*, January 11, 2011, http://english.peopledaily.com.cn/90001/90778/90859/7257326.html.

As previously discussed, most of this lending went to local governments and state-owned businesses. In June of 2011, the Chinese government revealed just how large the debts of the local governments were. The first national audit of regional finances published by Beijing showed that local governments owe RMB10,700 billion ($1.650 trillion). In theory, China's national debt is only 20% of GDP, a fraction of the debt of most Western countries and tiny compared to Japan's whopping 225%. However, if local debt and implicitly guaranteed loans are included, it would rise to well over 150% of China's GDP in 2010.[36]

Even worse, Beijing also has announced plans to bail out the local governments by assuming 2–3 trillion yuan ($308–463 billion). This confirms an estimate by Professor Victor Shih of Northwestern University that the bad debts on loans just to the local government will equal 25% of the total.[37] The total amounts of bad debt in the financial system could go much higher because many of these estimates do not include off-balance sheet loans that were very popular as a way to avoid government regulation, to say nothing of bad debts in the grey economy. According to Professor Shih, "The alarming thing is that no one, not even the central government, knows how much debt there is in the system."[38]

Needless to say, China has some real problems. As each day passes, the potential for a disaster increases. Many Chinese understand and admit it. According to Li Daokui, a professor at Tsinghua University and a member of the Chinese central bank's monetary policy committee, "The housing market problem in China is actually much, much more fundamental, much bigger than the housing market problem in the US and UK before your financial crisis," he said in an interview. "It is more than [just] a bubble problem."[39]

China could change, but given its present political system, change is almost certainly impossible. Leaders tend to repeat what has worked before. The only way to reliably bring in new ideas is generally to change leadership. All laws in every country, once established, form the basis of investment choices.

---

[36] Simon Rabinovitch and Jamil Anderlini, "Extent of Local Debts in China Laid Bare," *Financial Times*, June 27, 2011, www.ft.com.

[37] Dinny McMahon, "Victor Shih Sees Bank Bailout Redux," *wsj.com*, March 17, 2010, http://blogs.wsj.com/chinarealtime/2010/03/17/victor-shih-sees-bank-bailout-redux/?KEYWORDS=Victor+Shih.

[38] Tom Orlik, "China's Debt Burden Limits Policy Leeway," *Wall Street Journal*, March 9, 2011, http://online.wsj.com/article/SB10001424052748703883504576186252054344030.html?KEYWORDS=Victor+Shih.

[39] Geoff Dyer, "China Told Property Risk is Worse Than in US," *Financial Times*, May 31 2010, www.ft.com.

As a result, change may endanger profit. Policy inertia is both an economic and a political problem. The Chinese Communist Party has powerful incentives to maintain the present system.

Nonetheless, the belief in constant Chinese growth, the belief in spectacular profits from Chinese investments, and the belief in the inevitable shift of economic power continues. The mainstream US view continues to be that China's model might not be very moral or ethical, but it works. Conceivably, this assumption is so strong it will take another financial collapse before investors heed the warnings. In the meantime, markets continue to believe what former Federal Reserve Chairman Alan Greenspan said: "China is the most dynamic capitalist economy in the world."[40]

Investing in China

So, why, with the distorted financial information, would anyone want to invest in China? Without doubt, the financial information can be outright lies. The country's policies, although successful in the short run, in the end will inevitably result in a complete disaster. The reason people invest is simple: Wall Street and investors do not necessarily function on reality. Like Blanche Dubois in Tennessee Williams' *Street Car Named Desire*, investors "don't want realism. [They] want magic!" It is also an undeniable fact that some investors have profited handsomely from their Chinese stocks. While this is true, a lot has to do with their point of view. If investors look at their investments as long-term, sure bets, they could be courting disaster. In China, all illusions come with a "sell by" date.

Sina.com is one of China's three famous internet portals, which also include Sohu.com and Netease.com. Founded by Wang Zhidong, it was the darling of the market. What could be better than a combination of the internet, China, and new technology in a 1.3 billion-person market! The lure was irresistible. Initially priced at $17 per share, Sina.com's IPO was in the spring of 2000. Within a matter of weeks, it nearly doubled and continued to increase until reaching its high of $33 in late April 2000.

Nonetheless, there was a definite problem. To be an internet content provider in China, you needed permission from the Ministry of Information. An internet company must get the Ministry's approval before they receive foreign capital, cooperate with foreign businesses, or seek stock listings

---

[40] Maria Bartiromo, Interview with Alan Greenspan, CNBC.com, July 9, 2010, http://video.cnbc.com/gallery/?video=1540950189.

within China or abroad. Sina.com did not have Ministry approval. Instead, it had created a corporate structure that circumvented the regulations.

When Sina.com filed with the SEC in the United States, they detailed all of these arrangements in the documents. This is a step that the present trend for reverse mergers neatly allows companies to avoid. At that time, Chinese companies had to make the required disclosures in order to find a market. Sina.com pointed out, "We are restricted by the Chinese government from providing Internet and advertising services directly in China."[41] Furthermore, "Although the Company believes its business in China is in compliance with existing Chinese laws and regulations, the Company cannot be sure that the Chinese regulatory authorities will view such business as in compliance with Chinese laws and regulations."[42] Moreover, "Accordingly, it is possible that the relevant Chinese authorities could, at any time, assert that any portion or all of our existing or future ownership structure and businesses violate existing or future Chinese laws and regulations."[43]

But, of course, few read the prospectus and fewer still heeded the warning. Consequently, investors piled into Sina.com, the Chinese internet provider, which could not be a Chinese internet provider. Then the dot-com bubble burst. Everyone dumped. Sina went from $30 a share to $1.20 a share by October 2001, a decline of 96%.

Sina did bounce back, though, and it kept on bouncing. After a high of $45 in January of 2004, it fell again by 50% only eight months later. It then rode the Chinese stock market bubble in 2007 (which I accurately predicted[44]) to $56 and then fell to $19 with all the other equities in March 2009. But the "risk on" trade caused by the intersection of trillion dollar stimulus packages from both Beijing and Washington caused it to reach a new high of $147 in April of 2011.

Even though the stock hit new highs, the health of the company never lived up to expectations. The company has certainly grown. Sina is the top internet portal in the world's biggest internet market. It has a near-monopoly in China's rapidly growing micro-blogging world, and its version of Twitter—

---

[41] SinaCom, SEC, Form 10–Q, Quarterly Report, March 31, 2001, CIK number 0001094005, available at http://www.sec.gov/Archives/edgar/data/1094005/000109581101502076/f72554e10-q.txt20010514.

[42] Ibid.

[43] Ibid.

[44] William Gamble, "The Coming Crash in Chinese Stocks," *Financial Times*, May 15, 2007, http://www.ft.com.

Sina Weibo—has over 100 million users.[45] However, there is one huge problem. There are no profits. Although revenues were up 12% over the previous year and reached $105 million for the quarter, its losses were up as well. It lost $100 million. By June 2011, it had, once again, lost 50% of its value as it fell to $77 a share before rebounding. Despite the hype, Sina is anything but a sure thing. Although, if you were very patient and willing to put up with some heart-sickening fluctuations over a period of years, you would have made out very well; quite a lot depends on when you bought in and which bubble you rode.

Indirect Investment in China

Sina is, in many ways, a paradigm for indirect investors into China. In most market economies, there are millions of players each making different bets on the future. In China, there are millions of little players and one huge one, the government. So, what the government says goes. Many investors in China know this. So, rather than base their decisions on economic data or financial forecasts, they are very sensitive to government pronouncements. Worse still, government policy is intentionally a state secret. While most central banks and governments in developed countries strive for transparency, China tries very hard to limit any and all information.

The result is that the Chinese market can move very rapidly. Timing markets is extremely difficult. As Bernard Baruch once pointed out, "Don't try to buy at the bottom and sell at the top. It can't be done except by liars." Attempting to time the Chinese market is essentially impossible.

Not only can government policy change overnight, so can company information. Without the normal legal disincentives, the information that a company gives out can be completely false—as we saw with Sino-Forest. Reading the news won't help either. By the time the *Financial Times* or the *Wall Street Journal* publishes the information, the stock will have already fallen. If companies like Paulson and Carlyle are not privy to the information, an average investor certainly will not get it until it is too late.

Perhaps the only safe way to invest in China is to spread out the risk using exchange-traded funds (ETFs). One would assume that not all the companies that make up an ETF are going to be venal, or at least not venal in the same degree, so information about one should not force the entire sector to tank. But it will no doubt do damage.

---

[45] Josh Noble, "Sina: Still Waiting for Profits," *Financial Times*, March 2, 2011, http://www.ft.com.

Part of the problem with ETFs is that large state-owned companies dominate the portfolios. For instance, at least 40% of a sector fund, Global X China Energy ETF (CHIE), represents large state-owned companies. No doubt, though, the percentage is much higher. The Global X China Financials ETF (CHIX) is definitely 100% of state-owned companies. State-owned companies serve the state, so whether they make a profit or whether anyone knows about it does not necessarily interest management.

Energy companies illustrate this point. China controls its gas prices. If the government feels it is politically expedient, they have no problem in maintaining low prices at the pump and forcing the Chinese oil companies to take losses. This is a power of which American politicians can only dream! These perverse restrictions of a command economy can have contradictory results for the sector. Usually, when oil prices spike, energy company shares go up with them. In China, a rise in the global price of oil could result in losses.

China was able to spend its way out of the global recession, but not with direct taxpayer-funded stimulus. The Chinese financial companies represented in the ETF CHIX received orders to lend enormous amounts without regard to the quality of credit. The mounting bad loans on the books of Chinese banks may influence profits. Or they may not. It depends. Most likely, the government will keep the banks profitable by limiting the interest rates paid for deposits while keeping lending rates up. Increasing the "spread" will help the banks, but it will depress consumer spending. Whatever the government does or does not do, what investors must keep in mind is that the normal rules of finance and economics don't apply.

Another recent example of an artificial trend was in the rare earth bulge. Rare earth minerals are both key to and widely used in high-tech applications like wind turbines, car batteries, and a number of sophisticated defense applications.

China cornered the rare earth market by lowering costs enough to drive competitors out of business. They could have then reaped substantial profits by taking advantage of their monopoly and raising prices. But that would have been a market solution. Instead, the government simply informed the rest of the world that it would limit supply.

The result was similar to the Arab oil embargo. Prices spiked and will continue to do so for a short period of time. The government involvement forced the market to readjust by finding other sources of supply and limiting the use of rare earths with alternative technologies. Even worse, it has now encouraged other governments to subsidize production. The result will no doubt be a collapse of prices when other supplies come on line. The government rule also led to massive smuggling operations, which now make up an estimated 20% of the Japanese supply.

The point is that investors can make money by investing in these government-created distortions and bubbles provided they realize what they are. They are temporary and they are reversible. Furthermore, if kept in place long enough, they will result in a collapse. In order to time these markets, it is necessary to ignore the economic forecasts. An economic forecast makes certain assumptions about policy that are idiosyncratic to the person making the forecast. Instead, pay close attention to government pronouncements. It is not only important to pay close attention to what the government says, but also to realize it is often prudent to do the opposite. In a June 23, 2011, letter to the *Financial Times*, Premier Wen emphasized that all of the methods used by the Chinese government to tame inflation were working. Two weeks later, the inflation numbers came out, rising from 5.5% to 6.5%. As Sir Humphrey Appleby, the civil servant in the British parliamentary satire, *Yes, Minister,* pointed out, "Never believe anything until it's been officially denied."[46]

Another source for good information on China is to pay attention to certain commentators. The best include Professor Michael Pettis, an economist who teaches at Peking University's Guanghua School of Management. I have already mentioned Professor Yasheng Huang, who teaches political economy and international management at MIT Sloan School of Management. In addition, Andy Xie is very good. Although, until 2006, he was Morgan Stanley's star Asia-Pacific economist, an email that surfaced telling the truth cost him his job. The best journal is *Caixin Online*.

Try to avoid commentators with ties to investment banks or brokerages. Because they don't understand how a change in the rules changes everything, Western economists and financial writers tend to get the facts wrong when it comes to China. They consistently attempt to force historical data and economic theory developed from open market economies onto China—often in order to flog their wares. It doesn't work.

Direct Investment in China

Direct investors into China should pay close attention to the common wisdom about guanxi. Typically translated as relationships, most commentators view guanxi as some sort of cultural issue unique to the Chinese. It is not. It is simply a hallmark of a relationship-based system.

Guanxi is basic to doing business in China. Guanxi, for foreigners, is exceptionally difficult because, by definition, the networks are not transparent. You can never be sure who else is working with your partner or what your

---

[46] Jonathan Lynn, "Yes, Minister: Christmas Special: Party Games," 1984, http://www.jonathanlynn.com/tv/yes_minister_series/yes_minister_episode_quotes.htm.

partner owes or is owed. In a system without rules, time horizons shrink. Short-term profits are better than any long-term relationship. Laws are merely there for guidance. Attempting to enforce a contract or partnership agreement, or to protect intellectual property, is simply out of the question. You have to understand that the reason why prices for Bordeaux are so high is that there is enormous Chinese demand. Not that the Chinese actually drink the stuff, but a really expensive bottle of Bordeaux is considered appropriate currency for a bribe.

However, if your partner, and there has to be a partner of some sort, believes that he is better off with you than without you, then the business will work. Any business plan that involves selling into China has to ensure that your counterpart gets a really good deal from you. Otherwise, you will be expendable at the first opportune moment. One way to insure that you remain invaluable is to help the Chinese deal with the world. As difficult as it is for a Westerner to understand and deal with a relationship-based system, it is, in some ways, harder for the Chinese to understand and deal with a rule-based system. Helping them navigate and market to the rest of the world can reap huge benefits.

Still, any investor in China has to remember that the economic incentives for supplying the most important ingredient to making successful investments—accurate, timely, and complete information—is simply not there and is not going to be there. Also, things are not going to get better. There are few reasons for the people in charge to change the system; so, they won't.

Heed Mr. Market

Wu Jinglian is an economist. Known as "Mr. Market," in 2011 he is 81 and has struggled for forty years to promote a market economy. One of the original reformers, he has been a key advisor to China's leaders including Zhao Ziyang, and Zhu Rongji. In an interview with Chinese state television in January of 2001, he famously described the Chinese market as worse than a casino. "At least in a casino there are rules, like not peeping at others' cards," he said. "But in our stock market, some players can peep at others' cards—they can cheat."[47] Almost ten years later, although he is still at it, he recently "described the country's stock market as being in the 'age of robber barons' and pointed to insider trading by government officials as especially common."

---

[47] Richard McGregor, "Whistle Blower Tipped for Job with China's Fund Regulator," *Financial Times*, February 7, 2001, http://www.ft.com.

Most countries would laud a visionary economist who has done so much for China. Placed in a pantheon of the wise and good for their contributions to the country, they would be regarded as a true patriot and seen as one who fought for desperately needed change to heal the wounds inflicted by Mao and the Communist Party. Instead, the Chinese have another name for him: spy.[48] The reason he achieved this moniker was that he dared to challenge the China story. "In books, speeches, interviews and television appearances, he warns that conservative hardliners in the Communist Party have gained influence in the government and are trying to dismantle the market reforms he helped formulate."[49]

To make money in China, you have to listen to Mr. Wu and not to the Communist Party. You have to realize that it is not an ever-growing money machine run by technocrats and designed to create wealth for any foreigner willing to invest and with the patience to wait for the inevitable return. It is a very corrupt country with limited information about a string of ever-growing problems with few solutions. It is a relationship-based system designed to help those people running the country, the Communist Party, not foreign investors. If you understand this crucial point, you can keep your investment horizons very, very short. Ride the bubbles based on government policy and Party whim. If you are fortunate to make five or ten percent, great! Take your money off the table and leave the casino. Go home until the cycle repeats and then get back in. Nothing in China is a long-term bet. Quite the reverse.

Nearly a decade ago, in *Japan's Policy Trap*, Mikuni and Murphy wrote, "A century long policy of accumulating production capacity and claims on other countries without regard for profitability or return has saddled Japan with a huge pile of dollar assets. Those assets can neither be exercised nor exchanged without destroying the political economic base of the Japanese system, yet their sheer weight has defeated every attempt to restart the economy."[50] That sounds a lot like China to me.

---

[48] David Barboza, "China's Mr. Wu Keeps Talking," *New York Times*, September 27, 2009, http://www.nytimes.com/2009/09/27/business/global/27spy.html

[49] Ibid.

[50] Akio Miluni and R. Taggart Murphy, *Japan's policy trap: dollars, deflation, and the crisis of Japanese finance*, Brookings Institution Press, 2002, p. 189.

India

India has always been considered the poor cousin of China. In the 1980s, the Indian economy bumped along with a per annum growth rate below 4%. This slow economic growth led many forecasters, investors, and economists to deride India, and they assumed that its problems were due to cultural factors. Critics claimed India was stuck with a "Hindu growth rate" as if culture was related to economics.

Critics also saw a problem with India's political system. India has the world's largest democracy. It is vibrant, contentious, and often corrupt. In 2009, Indian citizens managed to elect 150 Members of Parliament (MPs) in the 15th Lok Sabha, the Indian parliament,[1] with criminal cases pending against them. This number represents 28% of the total number of 533 members.

India's government is dominated by two main parties, Congress and the Bharatiya Janata Party (BJP), but neither is ever able to secure a majority of seats. The result is often coalition governments that are beholden to small special-interest or regional parties with the power to veto important reforms.

Yet, despite these supposed impediments, India's economy has grown and rather fast. Democracies may be slow to act, but they have one major advantage over totalitarian states—they can change, sometimes rather quickly.

When India was founded in 1947, its rulers, including Nehru and his successors, believed in socialism as the best policy to attain fair and balanced

---

[1] "MPs with criminal charges aplenty in new House," *Hindu,* www.thehindu.com/2009/05/18/ stories/2009051860302000.htm, May 18, 2009.

growth. The instrument he used was a complex set of regulations know as the "License Raj." Under this system, a business, for example, would have to satisfy the requirements of up to 80 government agencies before beginning operations.[2]

All that changed in 1991 when India faced a balance-of-payments crisis. As part of the International Monetary Fund (IMF) bailout, the Indian government promised economic restructuring. The job was given to Finance Minister Manmohan Singh, who is presently India's Prime Minister.[3] Singh began a series of reforms that allowed India to start on a path to free up its market from the dead hand of government. While the process is far from complete, the developments so far have increased Indian economic growth to a level that almost competes with China's.

The Value of the Law

The economic growth in India, like the economic growth in China, proved one thing. Economic growth, the propensity to save, and entrepreneurial ability do not have anything to do with nationality or culture. They have to do with a country's law, whether in the form of regulations, economic policy, freedom of speech, or state ownership of large swaths of the economy. The difference between the legal infrastructures in some ways makes India the mirror image of China.

China's spectacular growth occurred as the result of fewer barriers. But this lack of impediments was not because the law was reformed or streamlined. It occurred because there was no law at all. Often commentators and economists admire the ability of Chinese technocrats to do whatever they want. They can because the government in China has unlimited power. It is not restricted by annoying laws. Want a new airport? Great! We will move 10,000 villagers and put them somewhere else. A new road? Fine, just point. Land for a factory? All yours, just as soon as we clear out a few peasants. Money? Here is a subsidized loan from the state-owned bank. No credit checks needed; just sign here. Cheap labor? Take your pick of expendable migrant labor. No protections, no unions, no problems.

India in contrast is filled with laws and regulations left over from the License Raj. So, any project can literally take years. South Korean steel-maker Posco,

---

[2] Wikipedia, "License Raj," http://en.wikipedia.org/wiki/Licence_Raj.

[3] Wikipedia, "Economic Liberalisation in India," http://en.wikipedia.org/wiki/Economic_liberalisation_in_India.

the world's third-largest steelmaker by output, wanted to build a $12 billion steel project in the Indian state of Orissa next to vast reserves of iron ore. After six years of navigating India's Byzantine government bureaucracy, Posco in 2011 finally secured all the requisite clearances for a proposed integrated steel plant, iron mine, and port in the eastern Indian state. But they still haven't been able to move a shovelful of earth because local villagers refuse to give up their lucrative livelihood, betel nut farming.

Of course, no betel nut farmers would ever get in the way of development in China, but the rights of the farmers, the legal rights, are something very, very important to all investors. Although India is still an emerging market with all of the hallmarks of other emerging markets, India, as Vodafone discovered, is different.

Choppy Indian Waters for Vodafone Reveals Investment Concerns

The British-based Vodafone Group Plc is the world's largest mobile telecommunications company based on revenues and the second largest based on the number of subscribers. China Mobile has about 522 million subscribers compared with Vodafone's 341 million. Vodafone dominates the European market and owns 45% of Verizon, the largest mobile telephone operator in the United States. Although it operates in over 30 countries and has partner networks in over 40 additional countries, before 2007 it did not have a presence in one of the largest markets in the world, India.

The Indian mobile telephone network is truly a prize worth winning. India is the world's second-largest mobile market after China based on subscribers. It has more than 600 million users, and that number grows by about 16 million customers a month. By 2015, the network is expected to have over 1.1 billion users.[4] Vodafone's growth in Europe and the United States was slowing, which is why India's emerging market story of rapid and seemingly unlimited growth potential was irresistible.

So, in 2007, Vodafone went looking for a potential acquisition candidate that would give it an entry into India. Since this is an emerging market, the candidate was owned by not one, but two powerful families, one in India and the other in Hong Kong. Hutchison Essar was the third largest mobile telephone company in India. Hutchison Telecommunications International (HTIL) of

---

[4]James Fontanella-Khan and James Lamont, "India vows action over licensing breaches," *Financial Times*, www.ft.com, November 19, 2010.

Hong Kong had a 66% stake in Hutchinson Essar. Hutchinson Telecom itself was a unit of Hutchison Whampoa, and Hutchison Whampoa is owned by the legendary Hong Kong tycoon, Li Ka-shing. Sir Li Ka-shing is the richest person in East Asia and the eleventh richest person in the world, with an estimated wealth of US$26 billion as of March 10, 2011.[5] Hutchison Whampoa is a conglomerate that spans everything from ports to real estate. It even holds a 0.8% share of Facebook.[6]

The Indian half of Hutchison Essar is 33% owned by Essar. Essar Group is one of India's biggest conglomerates. It is one of India's largest steel producers and has additional interests in energy, construction, ports, and communications. It has operations in more than 20 countries across five continents and revenues of $15 billion.[7] The company is also controlled by a family, the two brothers Shashi and Ravi Ruia, who jointly score fifth on *Forbes*'s list of the richest Indians.[8]

Vodafone was not alone in its interest of Li's share of Hutchison Essar. Essar made noises about purchasing the part of the company that it did not already own. The other serious potential bidder was another of India's family firms, Reliance Communications, which was at that time India's second-largest wireless operator. Reliance Communications is the flagship of Indian billionaire Anil Ambani's business. It is his share of the Reliance Empire built by his father, Dhirubhai Ambani. In a vehement battle between Anil and his brother Mukesh, which was settled only due to the intervention of their mother, Anil got telecommunications and financial services and Mukesh got the heavy industry, including hydrocarbons, petrochemicals, and polyester.[9]

The fight for Hutchison Essar was complicated by Indian law and Essar's contract. According to Indian law, if a telecoms company wants to buy another operator in the same network area, it must buy either 100% of the company or just 10%. This law meant that Reliance had to buy all or none of Hutchison Essar. The Ruias were not about to sell their share to a rival plutocrat. Besides, they had a right of first refusal regarding any purchase by an Indian company. This right, though, did not extend to foreign bidders like

---

[5] Wikipedia, "Li Ka-shing," http://en.wikipedia.org/wiki/Li_Ka-shing.

[6] Ibid.

[7] Wikipedia, "Essar Group," http://en.wikipedia.org/wiki/Essar_Group.

[8] Joe Leahy, "Essar to buy Trinity for up to $600m," *Financial Times*, www.ft.com, March 5, 2010.

[9] "The Ambani brothers: A durable yarn: A revealing account of India's most colorful business family," *Economist*, www.economist.com/node/17414013, November 4, 2010.

Vodafone. However, due to the laws restricting foreign investment for which India is famous, Vodafone's interest in an Indian telecommunications company could not exceed 74%. Vodafone needed an Indian partner.[10]

In the end, the deal went through. Vodafone made peace with the Ruias and was able to buy Li's share of Hutchison Essar. Vodafone was able to make the largest foreign investment in India's history. According to the deal, Ravi Ruia, the then vice-chairman of the minority shareholder Essar, would become chairman of the company, which was to be renamed Vodafone Essar, and Arun Sarin, Vodafone's Indian-born chairman, would become its vice-chairman.

Finally, on March 31, 2011, Vodafone said it had agreed to pay $5 billion to buy out the Essar Group in accordance with their contract, and both parties honored that contract. Vodafone was thereby able to raise its stake in the company up to the legal limit of 74%. The other 26% was to be owned by Indian investors.[11]

Since this saga happened in an emerging market, a bit of corruption occurred. Essar was involved in the Indian telecom scandal perpetrated by the telecom minister Andimuthu Raja in 2008. The infamous auction in 2008 allotted more of the spectrum to the two largest telecom companies—Bharti Airtel, India's biggest telecoms group by sales, and Vodafone—without paying charges. Auditors claim that the companies may be liable for more than $1 billion in retrospective fees.[12]

But Vodafone Essar wasn't the problem. The problem was Vodafone's partners, the Ruias. They had another iron in the fire, and this one turned out to be illegal.

In 2008, another Indian telecommunications company, Loop Telecom Pvt. Ltd, also applied for a license from telecom minister Andimuthu Raja. Under Indian law, one entity is barred from holding more than a 10% stake in two or more mobile operators in a service area. Through Essar, the Ruias already owned 33% stake in Vodafone Essar. They claimed that their interest in Loop was under the legal limit of 10%.

---

[10] Amy Yee and Sundeep Tucker, "New rival to Vodafone in Indian mobile bid," *Financial Times*, www.ft.com, December 28, 2006.

[11] "Kenan Machado Essar to Honor Pact With Vodafone," *Wall Street Journal*, http://online.wsj.com/article/SB10001424052748704415104576250691958536346 .html?KEYWORDS=Vodafone+and+Essar, April 8, 2011.

[12] James Fontanella-Khan, "Mobile groups pressed over 2G sell-off," *Financial Times*, www.ft.com, November 24, 2010.

What they failed to mention was that Loop Telecom Pvt. Ltd was originally named Shipping Stop Dot Com India Pvt. Ltd, which was owned by the Ruias and was ineligible for licenses, as it did not provide telecom services according to its incorporation documents and did not have the required paid-up capital to apply for the licenses. They also failed to mention that they had a sister, Kiran Khaitan, who also had a holding in Loop Telecom. But since this is an emerging market it was all in the family.

And there were a few other problems. First, in 2010, the intense competition created a price war that forced Vodafone to write off more than a quarter of the unit's book value from the previous year; second, a $2.5 billion pending tax liability was to be decided in the Indian Supreme Court in the summer of 2011.[13]

The real kicker is that after all of the money it has invested and the problems it has handled, Vodafone has not made a single rupee of profit. Still, the promise of emerging market growth is evident. Vodafone's Indian customers use more minutes than the rest of its network put together. Its Indian subscribers may generate less than $4 revenue each, but there are 139 million of them—about as many as Vodafone's Germany, Italy, and United Kingdom markets combined. In theory, India will soon allow consolidation. This will increase Vodafone's competitive advantage against the number-one provider in India, Bharti Airtel. Vodafone is now the second largest company in India and has a 24% share of the market, while Bharti Airtel has 28%. Both were able to add 2.45 million subscribers in May of 2011, but Vodafone was the only top-seven operator to make gains in every service area.[14]

Vodafone, like other investors in emerging markets, has made a very large bet on the future. It has navigated some rather large obstacles, like the dominance of family-owned businesses, corruption, crony capitalism, and its sometimes disparate and conflicting regulations. It has taken the company over four years and cost it at least $11 billion, not including recent investments. Depending on how the Indian Supreme Court rules, it could cost them over $2.5 billion more. In return for their investment, Vodafone has potentially one of the largest subscriber bases of any telecom company in the world. The question though, which is the most important question for investors in emerging markets, is whether after all the work, after all the problems, and after all the money, Vodafone will get to keep its investment. Investors definitely want a return on their investments, but they want their investments returned even more.

---

[13] Lex, "Vodafone in India: Worth the wait," *Financial Times*, www.ft.com, June 30, 2011.

[14] Ibid.

The Law Can Work . . . Eventually

Nathu Gaikwad is an investor, but he is certainly not in the same league as Vodafone. Not only can he not understand all of the complicated financial formulas that go into making modern global investment decisions, but also he can't read at all. He is an illiterate peasant from the Pune District in India. The Pune district is in the state of Maharashtra, which is 58 miles (93 kilometers) east of Mumbai.

Mr. Gaikwad's investment is what you would expect, land, 74 acres in fact. In 1986, he discovered a problem. The title to his property, or more accurately the property of his son-in-law's family, had been changed. The records had been forged, and the new owners were two businessmen.[15]

Changing records in India is quite a common scam. As India prospers, land nearer the cities becomes far more valuable for development. Rich developers bribe local officials to change the records so that the land of ignorant peasants can be made available for development. The same process goes on continually in China, where local governments confiscate the land of the local farmers and sell it to developers. In China, the farmers can only protest and riot, which they are doing constantly in ever growing numbers. Land is owned by the government and only leased to the users. But this is not China. It is India.

Mr. Gaikwad found out that he was not the only victim. According to Mr. Gaikwad, the "businessmen had allegedly indulged in similar fraudulent practices in the cases of several original title owners and grabbed vast tracts of land." So, Mr. Gaikwad turned to the Indian courts to retrieve his land.

Indian courts are notorious for their lack of speed. Intercontinental drift is sometimes considered faster. The number of cases pending before the Supreme Court stood at 43,580 in 2007, up from 19,806 in 1998. There are 3.7 million cases lodged in the High Courts and 25 million in lower courts.[16]

The courts are often corrupt as well. In a 2005 survey, it was estimated that the bribes paid to lawyers, police, and court officials equal around $580 mil-

---

[15] Vinita Deshmukh, "My name is Nathu Gaikwad. I may not be literate, but I used the RTI Act to get back land taken by land sharks," *MoneyLife*, http://foundation.moneylife.in/article/my-name-is-nathu-gaikwad-i-may-not-be-literate-but-i-used-the-rti-act-to-get-back-land-taken-by-land-sharks/12578.html, June 1, 2011.

[16] Jo Johnson, "Engaging India: Crisis in the courts," *Financial Times*, www.ft.com, September 6, 2007.

lion annually.[17] But the interesting part is that although slow, the courts do occasionally work.

India, like the United States, has a Supreme Court mandated by its constitution. The Supreme Court has appellate jurisdiction over the High Courts. Each state has a High Court, and the High Court has jurisdiction over the District Courts, which are located in each of a state's districts. An Indian district is similar to a county in the United States. In 1988, Mr. Gaikwad received a verdict from the High Court of Maharashtra, which directed the divisional commissioner to reinstate the original title of the land. But nothing happened.

As any lawyer anywhere knows, getting a judgment is only half the battle. Enforcing the judgment is another problem, especially in China, where the jurisdiction of the courts is limited to the province and sometimes just the city. A verdict in Shanghai could be meaningless in Chongqing. Unlike India, courts in China are a subsidiary and not a coequal branch of government. Court orders are often considered advisory and not mandatory. In contrast, in India, a court order must be obeyed. So, in theory at least, the county official should have complied with the court order resulting from Mr. Gaikwad's case. Instead, the officials in the land title office did nothing. They stated that the title could not be transferred back, because a case was pending in the lower District Court.

During his journey to find justice, Mr. Gaikwad was often asked for bribes to help expedite the process. He refused to pay them and instead persisted. In 2009, he used India's version of the Freedom of Information Act, the Right to Information Act (RTA), and asked for a copy of the official communication from the county official's office that had superseded the High Court order and the document showing that the matter was resting with the District Court. The local official responded that the document was "missing."

So, Mr. Gaikwad used the RTA again, this time at the state level. The State Information Commissioner ordered the county official to cough up the documentation or face criminal prosecution. What the county official finally produced was revealed as a forgery and a fake. So, after almost 20 years, it looks like Mr. Gaikwad will win his land back.

Cute story, but why should we care? Why should international businessmen and investors controlling billions of dollars bother with the story of some illiterate peasant fighting for some bit of Indian mud? Very simply, Mr. Gaikwad shows that, unlike China, India respects property rights, even if on a very basic level. So if Vodafone spends $11 billion and almost five years

---

[17] Ibid.

building up its business to something that is potentially very profitable, they get to keep it.

Property Rights in China vs. India

Contrast this with China. In the example of Sina.com we encountered an ownership structure where "it is possible that the relevant Chinese authorities could, at any time, assert that any portion or all of our existing or future ownership structure and businesses violate existing or future Chinese laws and regulations."[18] That was 11 years ago. This model became known as the Sina model, or "variable interest entity" (VIE). It works like this: valuable Chinese assets are placed in a Chinese company. This entity, the VIE, must be run by a Chinese citizen. A series of contracts are then arranged, shifting the returns from the VIE first to a foreign-owned company registered in China and then to an offshore company, perhaps in the Cayman Islands.[19]

Since the VIE ownership structure was seen as accepted law, it was used as the basis for billions of dollars of Western investment in China, and it is used by about half of the Chinese companies listed in America.[20] In March of 2011, authorities in Hebei "declared that the very existence of a VIE contravened Chinese management and public policies."[21]

There is an ongoing dispute between Yahoo! and its Chinese partner, Alibaba. Yahoo! owns 43% of Alibaba through a VIE. Alibaba just transferred a very valuable asset of Alibaba, Alipay, an online-payments firm, to a local Chinese company controlled by Jack Ma, Alibaba's chairman. Yahoo! is understandably outraged by this theft, but Mr. Ma claimed that he had no choice and that the People's Bank of China required that Alipay had to be in a wholly owned Chinese company to operate.[22]

Of course, these little outrages do not mean that big foreign firms will suddenly find that their investments in China are illegal or worthless. The Chinese government would never, ever do that. Or would they?

---

[18] SinaCom, SEC, Form 10-Q, Quarterly Report, March 31, 2001, CIK number 0001094005, www.sec.gov/Archives/edgar/data/1094005/000109581101502076/f72554e10-q.txt20010514.

[19] "China's murky ownership rules: Who owns what? The perils of investing where the law is unclear," *Economist*, www.economist.com/node/18928526, July 7, 2011.

[20] Ibid.

[21] Ibid.

[22] Ibid.

China has been feeling its oats recently. For historical reasons, beginning with the humiliation of the opium wars in the nineteenth century to the atrocities committed by the Japanese in the twentieth century, foreigners are not all that popular in China. They were tolerated because of the money and technology they brought that helped China develop. However, there is a rising belief that China has progressed to the point where it no longer needs them. One thing for sure: in China Mr. Gaikwad wouldn't find his property protected by the law.

Indirect Investment in India

India has two stock exchanges: The Bombay Stock Exchange (BSE) and the National Stock Exchange of India (NSE). Together their market capitalization is about $3 trillion, less than half of China's total, but closing in on the total of London and of Tokyo.[23] Unlike many emerging markets, India does not have a stock exchange that was founded within the last twenty years. The Bombay Stock Exchange is actually quite old. It was founded 135 years ago. Like other emerging markets, the size of India's exchanges has exploded. The nation's two exchanges have seen a nearly 10-fold increase in their combined market value in the past decade.[24] In 2009 and 2010, foreign investors poured more than $45 billion into Indian stocks.[25]

Like most emerging markets, India has a securities watch dog—the Securities and Exchange Board of India, generally known by its acronym SEBI. It was initially established in 1992 but not given any powers until 1995. US securities law, embodied in the Securities Act of 1933 and the Securities Exchange Act of 1934, have had an enormous effect on securities laws throughout the world, and nowhere more so than India. The law governing SEBI is almost identical to the one in the United States. This is common. India is a common law jurisdiction that not only shares a similar legal system with the United States, but it sometimes cites US law as precedent.

SEBI does not have the glaring conflicts of interest that the Chinese watchdog, the CSRC, suffers. While there are many state-owned companies listed on Indian stock exchanges, the number is a small fraction relative to the total number. Compare this to to China, where most, if not all, of the companies listed on the exchanges are state-owned.

---

[23] Wikipedia, "List of stock exchanges," http://en.wikipedia.org/wiki/List_of_stock_exchanges.

[24] Romit Guha, "Debate on Indian Exchange Regulations Heats Up," *Wall Street Journal*, December 29, 2010.

[25] Ibid.

Nonetheless, SEBI is not without problems. For several years leading up to the 2008 crash, the SEC's enforcement was definitely lacking and SEBI was no different. For example, in 2006, India was rocked with a scandal. A group of market manipulators were able to corner large chunks of the retail investment quotas of initial public offerings. They were permitted to do so by banks, registrars, brokers, and the National Securities Depository Ltd (NSDL). All of these intermediaries were indicted, but only the banks and other intermediaries were punished. NSDL was not.[26]

NSDL decided to contest the issue. Fortunately for the company, its president, C.B. Bhave, was later appointed by the government as the chairman of SEBI. To avoid any political fallout, the government appointed a two-member panel of other SEBI board members to investigate NSDL and decide upon its guilt.

The panel included Dr. Mohan Gopal, who had taught at Harvard Law School in the United States for over a decade. Rather than exonerate NSDL, Dr. Gopal issued a report that upheld some charges and questioned why NSDL's systems were not robust enough to detect the scam. Instead of acting on the report, SEBI suppressed it and voided the orders against NSDL.

In protest, Dr. Gopal wrote a letter to the Indian Prime Minister, charging that an "informal clique of current and serving bureaucrats, SEBI officials, lawyers and corporate interests orchestrated a subversion of the due process of law."[27] And there the matter would have rested, except for the Right to Information Act that we met in the story of Mr. Gaikwad. Using the RTA, the letter was unearthed and published. SEBI was forced to reverse its actions.

Like the effect of the Madoff scandal on the SEC, the NSDL issue will hopefully lead to further reforms in the SEBI. But like the story of Mr. Gaikwad, the moral is that the problems with SEBI and its ability to regulate the market did surface through the use of the law, which is important because India definitely needs a more effective regulator.

The real problem with India's securities market is one that it shares with other emerging markets. It tends to be shallow, illiquid, and concentrated in the hands of a few individuals. Interestingly, the problem has gotten worse as India's market has expanded. In India, the retail participation in the stock

---

[26] Sucheta Dalal, "Unaccountable regulators: Cancerous caucus," *MoneyLife*, http://foundation.moneylife.in/article/unaccountable-regulators-cancerous-caucus/12603.html, June 9, 2011.

[27] Ibid.

market has declined from 20 million investors in the 1990s to around 8 million in 2009, according to official data. This decline occurred despite a 2000% growth in market capitalization. Retail investor participation is just 1.3% in India in contrast to the United States, where it is 27.7%.[28]

Worse, small numbers of investors control the market. From April to June 2010, 50% of the cash market transactions on the NSE came from a shockingly low number of investors, 451, of whom 156 were proprietary traders. Even fewer investors traded derivatives. Over 50% of the trading in NSE's derivatives segment came from just 106 investors, of whom 58 were proprietary traders.[29] According to the *Economist*, "Indian 'promoters' (who include business families and other corporate insiders) still hold almost half of the shares on the National Stock Exchange (NSE)."[30]

With so few traders, there is enormous possibility for insider trading and price manipulation. Take for example the listed company Westlife Development. This is a company in India that offers investment and financial services. Its sales deteriorated for most of 2009, and the company went into the red by December—hardly a recommendation for spectacular growth, though its stock price certainly rose. From January 1, 2009, to April 27, 2010, the stock grew 4307%![31] But Westlife is hardly alone. In 2010, several stocks experienced similar rises: Supertex Industries, 4140%; Veritas India, 3227%; Prism Informatics, 3149%; Polygenta Technologies, 2190%; Neha International, 1509%; and Nikki Global Finance, 1169%.[32]

What concerns investors, though, are not the rises but the falls. Some of the falls have been just as spectacular as the rises. The movement is not only due to market manipulators. As in all emerging markets, many companies in India have succeeded because of strong political connections. The difference in India is that because of a lively press, the world tends to find out about these scandals. Two large firms, Sun TV and the budget carrier SpiceJet, crashed by

---

[28] Moneylife Digital Team, "Increasing retail investor base: SEBI has a tough job ahead," *MoneyLife*, www.moneylife.in/article/increasing-retail-investor-base-sebi-has-a-tough-job-ahead/16977.html, June 2, 2011.

[29] Ibid.

[30] "Offshore inmates: India struggles to get to grips with a bewildering corporate fraud," *Economist*, www.economist.com/node/12943984, January 15, 2009.

[31] *MoneyLife*, www.moneylife.in/article/6280.html, June 3, 2010.

[32] Devarajan Mahadevan and Pratibha Kamath, "Insider trading: Why has it taken SEBI so long to wake up?," *MoneyLife*, www.moneylife.in/article/72/11167.html, , November 15, 2010. Note: this article contains the urls to articles specifically about each stock.

over 27% and 16% respectively in June of 2011 after an exposé in the famous muckraking newspaper *Tehelka*.[33]

All of these scandals and the sometimes relaxed attitude of the regulator may seem to some to be reasons to avoid indirect investing in India. On the contrary, they are exactly the reason to invest in India. India does in fact meet the promise of an emerging market. Emerging markets will continue to achieve their promise if and only if market reforms continue. If you do not know what is wrong, you can't fix it. If you don't know where the trouble is, you can't avoid it. If you don't know what the risks are, you cannot hedge them.

The general perception in the market is that when India's lively press exposes a scandal, that means the market should be avoided. Instead, exposés help investors know what to avoid. As capital is allocated to companies with more transparency and better governance, the market has a strong economic incentive to improve. In contrast, such incentive does not exist in China. A prominent Chinese government-owned business newspaper, the *Economic Times*, disbanded its investigative muckraking reporting team.[34]

There is hope for the future in India, but the present situation can be unstable. The best way, then, to invest in India again would be the use of ETFs. ETFs spread out the risk of manipulation and false information across a broader spectrum of equities and so lessen the impact. The problem with ETFs is that they are designed for and marketed mostly to developed market investors. Both the sponsors of the ETFs and the purchasers assume that a given investment strategy for developed markets is the same for emerging markets.

For example, in developed markets, there are many "small cap" ETFs. The theory behind such funds is that, according to long-term market data, smaller companies grow slightly faster than larger companies. Of course, there are many caveats to such theories—like what constitutes the period and the definition of a "small cap"—but at least intuitively it makes sense. These funds are not limited to the United States. There are also small cap funds for Canada, Australia, Europe, and Japan.

---

[33] Moneylife Digital Team, "Perils of investing in companies growing through political links," *MoneyLife*, http://202.154.165.233/article/perils-of-investing-in-companies-growing-through-political-links/16980.html, June 3, 2011.

[34] Josh Chin, "Beijing State Newspaper Closes Its Investigative Team," *Wall Street Journal*, http://online.wsj.com/article/SB10001424052702304567604576453723875263218.html?mod=djemITPA_h, July 19, 2011.

The problem is with small cap funds in emerging markets. There are small cap funds for India, China, Brazil, Taiwan, and Korea. There's even a generic emerging market of small cap funds, which is absurd. Small companies in Korea have nothing to do with small companies in China or India, and they certainly are not like small companies in the United States. This is again a recurrent problem. Financial firms, analysts, and economists are constantly using developed-world tools to understand emerging markets. They have no idea that when the rules change, so does the game.

In Korea, the dozen or so *chaebol*s dominate most industries. Although smaller firms in Korea provide 90% of the jobs, they are usually very small, like family-owned restaurants. Their numbers are also dwindling. They used to make up 55.8 % of the economy, but that has shrunk to 52.6%.[35] The reality is that they cannot really compete against the *chaebol*s, which are now being restricted from entering certain areas of business in Korea. The list gives you some idea of the size of these businesses: soap, light bulbs, industrial molds, satellite receivers, bottles, sunglasses, toys, and vacuum cleaners.[36] Occasionally a small business is successful. When that happens it is snapped up by one of the *chaebol*s.

Small-to-medium-sized businesses (SMEs) in emerging markets have enormous problems accessing capital. Most of the banks prefer to lend to the larger companies, which are either owned by the state or powerful families. Many SMEs are forced to borrow money from underground money lenders.

The Chinese province of Zhejiang is known for its small entrepreneurial companies, especially in the city of Wenzhou. As of the summer of 2011, interest rates from underground banks had reached 10% a month—over 20 times the 6.5% per annum charged by state banks. As a result, more than 7,300 companies in Zhejiang were forced to close.[37] Closing in China does not mean bankruptcy, however, because bankruptcy basically does not exist. In China, closing is more literal. It usually means that the owner removes whatever assets he can, closes and locks the doors, and leaves town. Investors and former employees get nothing.

There are likely to be more closures. According to a report sent to the State Council by the All China Federation of Industry and Commerce, the

---

[35] Christian Oliver, "Seoul tells chaebol sharks to leave small fry," *Financial Times,* www.ft.com, September 21, 2010.

[36] Christian Oliver, "Seoul bolsters small companies in 'tofu war'," *Financial Times,* www.ft.com , July 18, 2011.

[37] Daniel Ren, "Higher loan shark interest hurting firms," *South China Morning Post,* http://topics.scmp.com/news/china-business-watch/article/Higher-loan-shark-interest-hurting-firms, July 18, 2011.

official chamber of commerce for non-state companies, 7.5 million SMEs have been hit hard by Beijing's recent credit tightening. The credit tightening was supposed to cool inflation, but state-owned banks throughout the recession have preferred to lend to large state-owned enterprises rather than small companies. The report, the product of a three-month survey of private businesses in 17 provincial-level regions, showed that SMEs were in "even worse shape" than at the beginning of the recession in 2008.[38]

There is a joke about India, where cricket is the favorite sport. The joke is that Indians can never play games like soccer (football elsewhere) that are played on a rectangle, because someone will set up a shop in a corner. India, perhaps more so than other emerging markets, is teeming with smaller entrepreneurial companies. But these small companies have just as much trouble borrowing money from a state-dominated banking system as other small companies throughout the emerging markets. Also, if a small company is listed, its stock is much more likely to be subject to manipulation. The level of corporate governance in small companies in all emerging markets leaves much to be desired. These are all family-owned companies that will always favor the family.

India is home to some first-rate, world-class companies that meet international standards, especially in the IT sector. Companies like Wipro and Infosys compare favorably with their competitors in the United States. But for every Wipro, there is also a Satyam, which imploded after an accounting scandal. So, there is a suspicion that the exceptional performance of the large family-controlled groups that dominate the BSE index of 30 leading shares and make up any index tracked by an ETF might result from artful bookkeeping or political connections.[39] So, for India and most emerging markets, a broad-based ETF would both reflect India's growth potential and limit risks associated with a given company.

Direct Investment in India

As the Vodafone study shows, it is possible to make inroads into an enormous market. The process does take patience, and there are many obstacles. One important factor in making direct investments in India is to understand the real situation and avoid some of the hype.

---

[38] Ren Wei, "SMEs heading for financial collapse, Beijing warned," *South China Morning Post*, www.scmp.com/portal/site/SCMP/menuitem.2af62ecb329d3d7733492d9253a0a0a0/?vgnextoid=267ca8d809d41310VgnVCM100000360a0a0aRCRD&ss=World&s=Business, July 22, 2011.

[39] Lex, "Indian corporate governance," *Financial Times*, www.ft, January 12, 2009.

For example, people like Thomas Friedman, in his extremely successful book *The World is Flat*, conjured an image of billions of cheap, well-educated, English-speaking workers that could be employed to lower overhead in any market. It simply isn't true.

Take for example the idea of millions of graduates. Yes, it is true that India graduates millions of prospective employees, but few actually have the skills that a direct investor would want. A call center in Bangalore has openings for 3,000 employees, but it cannot fill the vacancies. "So few of the high school and college graduates who come through the door can communicate effectively in English, and so many lack a grasp of educational basics such as reading comprehension, that the company can hire just three out of every 100 applicants."[40] There are seats for 1.5 million students, nearly four times the 390,000 available in 2000, but 75% of technical graduates are unemployable.[41]

The problem is not only that the education system is not turning out qualified employees. There is also some corruption in the academic system, although probably not as bad as in China, where all sorts of academic fraud is widespread and where "poor peer-review mechanisms, misguided incentives and a lack of checks on academic behavior all allow fraud to be more common."[42]

Taking advantage of semi-skilled and unskilled labor is also very difficult in India. China was able to take advantage of its large population to feed the needs of foreign manufacturers, basically because it had few, if any, restrictions on labor. Not so in India.

Gandhi was able to get rid of the British with help from labor unions. In exchange, India passed a labor code that was more appropriate for a developed European country than an emerging market. The Industrial Disputes Act of 1947 makes hiring and firing very difficult. Size restrictions on Indian companies have kept them relatively small; 87% of manufacturing jobs are with companies that employ fewer than ten people.[43] So, although the wages in India are far below those of even China, the country cannot take advantage of the low costs. Ironically, Indian companies, like their Western counterparts, had to become more capital intensive to avoid the restrictions,

---

[40] Geeta Anand, "India Graduates Millions, but Too Few Are Fit to Hire," *Wall Street Journal*, http://online.wsj.com/article/SB1000142405274870351550457614420 92863219826.html?mod=djemITPA_h#printMode, April 5, 2011.

[41] Ibid.

[42] "Academic fraud in China: Widespread academic fraud may hamper a drive for innovation," *Economist*, www.economist.com/node/16646212, July 22, 2010.

[43] "An elephant, not a tiger," *Economist*, www.economist.com/node/12749735, December 11, 2008.

which is one of the many reasons why India, unlike China, has created many companies that are competitive globally.

The paradox of India is the law, or, more precisely, an economically inefficient legal infrastructure. According to Arvind Virmani, former Chief Economic Advisor in the Indian Ministry of Finance and India's representative for the International Monetary Fund, India needs to reform. India needs "fiscal reform, including of subsidies; privatization of public enterprises; opening state-controlled banks to more private ownership; reform of India's throttling labour laws; and liberalizing certain industries, including coal and sugar." Of course, he made these suggestions in a book published in 1999, and they still have not been followed. With the exception of labor laws, China has not reformed any of these areas either, but there the similarities end.[44]

One thing is exceptionally clear to the voters in India. Reform has helped their country grow and provided economic security for millions of people. Many of these people have a growing stake in a growing India, and they understand that a growing India means change. Consequently, for economic reasons, democratic India will be motivated to change its laws to make them more efficient. In contrast, much of the way China operates, including its incredibly imbalanced and unsustainable economy, works very well for the state and the Communist Party who runs it. The real estate bubble supported by cheap loans and the export industry supported by the cheap yuan help local governments and state-owned industries. So, there is no motivation to change a system that has kept the party in power and made many members exceptionally rich. As a result, authoritarian China will not change, also for economic reasons.

---

[44] "A survey of India: Storm-clouds gathering, What the world recession will do to India's economy," *Economist*, www.economist.com/node/12749795, December 11, 2008.

Russia

It is hardly surprising that Jim O'Neill chose to include Russia as part of the BRICs. Russia has enormous potential, partially due to its size. The Russian land mass makes it the largest country in the world, and it ranks 10th in population. Its economy is large as well. In terms of nominal GDP, it is 11th behind India, China, Brazil, and the G7 countries.[1] In terms of purchasing power parity, it ranks ahead of the UK, France, Italy, and Brazil.

The country is also awash with natural resources. It has the eighth-largest oil reserves, with over 5% of the world supply. It also has the world's largest reserves of natural gas but its natural resources do not stop at hydrocarbons. It also has large supplies of nickel, tin, diamonds, aluminum, and even gold.[2]

Besides natural resources, Russia has a well-developed infrastructure. Its rail network is second only to the United States. In terms of its road network, it ranks eighth. It is the sixth-largest producer of wheat in the world and ranks third in its amount of arable land.[3]

It is not only its resources that provide the basis for growth. Africa has much of the world's resources but is famous mostly for its poverty. To insure growth, you must have an educated population, and Russia does. It has

---

[1] Canada, France, Germany, Italy, Japan, the United Kingdom, and the United States.

[2] World Mining Production Figures | Mineral Mining Industry, www.economywatch.com/mineral/, April 30, 2010.

[3] NationMaster.com, www.nationmaster.com/country/rs-russia/edu-education.

an exceptionally high literacy rate. It ranks fourth in both tertiary education enrollment and parity in literacy rates between men and women.[4]

In its drive to compete with the West, the old communist government of the Soviet Union gave Russia everything it needed to be a first-rate superpower, except one thing. Like the Communist Party in China, the communist government of the Soviet Union destroyed all of Russia's institutions. After its collapse, there were few institutions remaining that were capable of turning a relationship-based system into a rule-based system. There were no laws or courts to limit the power first of the oligarchs and then of the *siloviki* (strong guys). The siloviki, alumni of the security services, were appointed by Putin to run state companies and ministries and take back the country's richest assets from the oligarchs and put them under the control of the state. The problem is that they ran their assigned departments as personal fiefdoms, handing out patronage, ignoring corruption, and dividing the spoils among themselves.

Recently, President Dmitry Medvedev and his band of former economists, lawyers, and bankers, so-called *slaboviki* (weak guys), have been cleaning house. The number of siloviki in government has declined from 66% in 2007 to 27% in 2010. On March 31, 2011, the most powerful of all, Igor Sechin, deputy prime minister and one of the most powerful men in Russia, was fired from the state oil company, Rosneft.[5] But, despite the efforts, much remains the same. The country's top 70 officials have not changed at all under Mr. Medvedev.[6]

The result is a system based almost totally on relationships and political connections. For those who are connected, like the princelings in China, vast riches are available for them and their families. The 25-year-old daughter of the governor of Sverdlovsk province in the Urals co-founded and made an investment of 126 million rubles ($4.5 million USD) in a timber mill.[7] The head of the Federal Security Service has a son who is president of the northwest regional branch of VTB, the second-largest bank in Russia. A scion of the chairman of Russia's National Security Council is the president of Rosselkhozbank, another of the country's largest lenders.[8]

---

[4] Ibid.

[5] Charles Clover, "Politics: Shift in focus puts former spies out in the cold," *Financial Times*, www.ft.com, April 27 2011.

[6] Charles Clover, "Russia: Ascent and dissent," *Financial Times*, www.ft.com, July 11, 2011.

[7] Ibid.

[8] Ibid.

For the connected, the system is great. For those who are not so fortunate, it is stifling. The lack of opportunity prevents Russia from capitalizing on one of its most important resources, educated people. Sadly, they are simply leaving. The worst part is that the emigrants are the best educated. Millions of scientists and computer programmers have left since the collapse of the Soviet Union. They are still leaving at the rate of about 100,000 a year.[9]

The reasons have changed. Emigration used to be solely economic. But real wages have doubled in less than a decade under former President Vladimir Putin.[10] Now the reason for leaving is frustration with the system. Surveys by the Levada Center, an independent research institute in Moscow, found a similar broad trend. According to a recent survey, the number of people, mostly young people, thinking of leaving has risen to 44%.[11] The well-educated readers of the *Novaya Gazeta*, a newspaper famous for its investigative coverage, with four dead journalists to prove it, were even more adamant about getting out: 62% wanted to go.[12] They wanted to go because of the quality of life.

The state controls television news, film, and even the pop music scene. According to one well-connected, young, successful Russian, it takes "10 to 20 years to buy a flat, or five years to buy a car. There are no chances for promotion. It's very hard to set up your own business. Loans cost 20% to 30% a year."[13]

The once great Russian education system has been totally corrupted. Anything from placement in schools to university degrees is available for a price. The health care system is hardly any better. It is also insular. Although Russian graduates teach around the world, Russia has few, if any, foreign professors.[14]

It is not only Russia's human capital that is being wasted. Its vast natural resources, instead of being an engine for economic growth, are only a piggy

---

[9] Ibid.

[10] Charles Clover, "Rivalry at the top causes unease," *Financial Times*, www.ft.com, April 27, 2011.

[11] Julian Evans, "Why Are They Leaving? Russia's small but educated middle-class is deserting the mother country in search of opportunities and freedoms elsewhere, but the state is waking up to their grievances and reform could be in the air," *The Wall Street Journal*, http://online.wsj.com/article/SB100014240527487048166045763330302459349 82.html?KEYWORDS=JULIAN+EVANS, June 16, 2011.

[12] Ibid.

[13] Ibid.

[14] Konstantin Sonin, "Universities Need to Hire From Outside," *The Moscow Times*, www.themoscowtimes.com/opinion/article/universities-need-to-hire-from-outside/203439.html, August 1, 2006.

bank for the corrupt. Transparency International ranked 44 companies that accounted for 60% of global oil and gas production on their anti-corruption programs. It was hardly surprising that Gazprom scored a zero.

Gazprom owns 25% of the world's natural gas reserves, yet it barely makes a profit. It sells more gas every year at higher prices but, for some reason, its expenses seem to grow at a much faster rate. In 2008, for example, Gazprom increased its operating budget so much that there was a question about its management's motives. According to the Russian research firm Troika Dialog, "This raises questions about whether the management actually intends to generate any meaningful free cash flow."[15] Again in 2011, Gazprom managed to pare back a tripling of profits for most of 2010 by a 12% increase in operating costs.

The increase in operating costs usually has to do with the purchase of oil and gas from shady 'intermediaries' or no-bid contracts awarded to politically connected firms. Both of these methods allow for the significant skimming of revenues from this state-owned firm.

Russia is typical of many commodities-exporting countries. They have what is known as the "curse of oil." The huge amounts of money that flow into many resource-rich countries with weak institutions often only flow to the corrupt elite, whose economic incentive as *rentiers* is only to increase their share. Since there are few, if any, legal or institutional limits on the amount they can take, they usually try to take it all. Small wonder that rental rates for luxury shops on Moscow's exclusive shopping street Stoleshnikov Pereulok are just behind those in London or Paris.[16]

But the curse of oil has another perverse effect. It prevents the economy from producing jobs for a skilled workforce. According to Mikhail Chernysh of the Russian Academy of Science's Institute of Sociology, "Russia is an oil and gas exporting economy, and oil and gas production does not require large amounts of highly qualified labour. Only 15 per cent of jobs are highly skilled, so under present circumstances that is the largest that the middle class can be."[17]

It is not just the Russians who have problems with the system. Foreign investors seeking to cash in on Russia's mineral wealth face innumerable obstacles, as the British oil major, BP, discovered.

---

[15] "Gazprom Drops 4% on 'Shocking' Spending Plan," *The Moscow Times*, August 25, 2008.

[16] "Luxury Shop Rents at Global Highs," *The Moscow Times*, www.themoscowtimes.com/print/article/luxury-shop-rents-at-global-highs/441084.html, July 26, 2011.

[17] Charles Clover, "Russia: Ascent and dissent," *Financial Times*, www.ft.com, July 11, 2011.

The riches of the Russian oil market have been an enormous temptation for Western oil companies since the fall of the former Soviet Union. These are some of the most powerful, largest, and best-connected companies in the world. Since beginning, they have explored and found oil in some of the most geologically, environmentally, and politically inhospitable places on the planet. For the most part they succeeded, but not in Russia.

Not that they haven't tried. Shell was developing several oil and gas fields off Sakhalin Island in Russia's Far East along with Japanese partners. In 2006, the $22 billion project was cited for various violations of environmental regulations. Rather than continue in a war that it could not win, Shell took the offer and sold out to Gazprom.[18]

BP, on the other hand, has been in Russia a lot longer. Its Russian entity, TNK-BP, was formed in 2003 at a ceremony attended by then President Putin.[19] TNK is a vertically integrated Russian oil group that was part of the spoils from the Yeltsin privatization program. It was owned by a partnership of oligarchs called AAR. One oligarch, Mikhail Fridman, owns Alfa Group. Another, Len Blavatnik, owns Access Industries. A third, Viktor Vekselberg, owns Renova, which provides the R in AAR.

All of these companies own vast amounts of property all over the world in a variety of industries. As usual, these are family-owned businesses. Their owners are past masters of navigating the relationships inherent in post-Soviet Russia. They have an intricate web of connections throughout the halls of power within the Kremlin. They are well aware of the limits placed on them by the system in which they operate and are very careful not to transgress the rules. The same cannot be said for their new partner, BP.

By 2004, BP was quite happy with its new partnership. So happy, in fact, that its CEO at the time, Lord John Browne, "insisted that the political risk he faced in Russia was no greater than anywhere else."[20] He was wrong. In February 2005, the Russian government decided that if anyone was going to skim profits from Russian oil, it was going to be politicians and not foreigners. So they banned majority ownership by foreigners of many new natural resource concessions. By April, they wanted more and hit TNK-BP with a $1 billion tax bill. Then the problems started.

---

[18] Henry Meyer, "Russia Repels Retailers as Ikea Halt Curtails Medvedev Goal," *Bloomberg,* www.bloomberg.com/news/2011-03-01/russia-repels-retailers-as-ikea-halt-curtails-medvedev-bric-goal.html, March 2, 2011.

[19] "BP and Russia: Russian arm twisting Another energy firm backs down," *The Economist,* www.economist.com/node/9390152, June 22, 2007.

[20] "Global or national? The perils facing Big Oil," *The Economist,* www.economist.com/node/3884594, April 28, 2005.

One of the main contributions made by the AAR partnership to TNK-BP was the Kovykata gas field in eastern Siberia. The license owned by TNK-BP required that the company increase production quotas, which BP was happy to do, but any increase had nowhere to go. The company responsible for the pipelines was the huge, state-owned gas company, Gazprom. Gazprom also had a monopoly on exports and had not built the pipelines necessary for international sales. Since TNK-BP could not meet the specifications within their license agreement, the authorities threatened to cancel the license. The courts were useless, so TNK-BP agreed to sell its stake in Kovykata to Gazprom for about $800 million.[21] Then BP's Russian ventures hit some bumps.

In 2008, BP's Russian partners decided that they had different ideas as to where TNK-BP should go. BP saw the partnership as a large part of its global business, basically a subsidiary. After all, TNK-BP represented 25% of BP's production and 40% of its replacement reserves.[22] In contrast, AAR felt that TNK-BP was a separate company. They wanted it to branch out and compete internationally. This would have caused several issues for BP.

First, the partnership, instead of being a piggy bank, would have competed directly with BP. Second, BP has a large business presence in the United States. It has been the largest supplier of oil to the US military, selling almost a billion dollars of product in 2009.[23] The Russians also wanted to do deals in Cuba, Iran, and Syria. These deals would have been illegal under US law because the countries are blacklisted by the US Department of State. The Russian partners felt that "TNK-BP is an independent Russian company and should be subject to Russian laws."[24]

The Russian shareholders had a valid point. Normally in these disputes, hoards of lawyers pick over the minutiae of the agreement, followed by negotiations and, in the worst case, litigation. Eventually the dispute would be settled, usually without intervention of a court. But this is Russia. They do it differently. In Russia you know there is a problem when your offices are raided by a mass of weapons-toting, balaclava-wearing security police. You

---

[21] "BP and Russia: Russian arm twisting another energy firm backs down, *The Economist,* June 22, 2007.

[22] "Business in Russia: Crude tactics—The curious goings-on at TNK-BP are even stranger than they appear," *The Economist,* www.economist.com/node/11502165, June 5, 2008.

[23] R. Jeffrey Smith, "BP has steady sales at Defense Department despite U.S. scrutiny," *The Washington Post,* www.washingtonpost.com/wp-dyn/content/article/2010/07/04/AR2010070403632.html, July 5, 2010.

[24] "Business in Russia: Crude tactics—The curious goings-on at TNK-BP are even stranger than they appear," *The Economist,* www.economist.com/node/11502165, June 5, 2008.

also don't get served with notice of pending litigation. You find out about it when you receive an injunction from an obscure court in Siberia.

BP's offices in Moscow were raided on a charge of industrial espionage. A small brokerage firm in Moscow called Tetlis secured an injunction from a court in Siberia barring payments to BP-related contractors and barring staff from TNK-BP offices. Foreign staff were subject to inspections for labor violations. Senior staff has had their visas denied. TNK-BP's CEO Robert Dudley, who was appointed by BP, was called in for questioning in a tax evasion probe.[25] The Russian partners, of course, denied that they had anything to do with the harassment.

Eventually Dudley had to resign, which left TNK-BP without a CEO. Two years later, the partners finally agreed on a 35-year-old Russian oil executive, Maxim Barsky. Mr. Barsky is a graduate of St. Petersburg University and holds an MBA from UC Berkley. He had run West Siberian Resources, one of Russia's most successful independent oil companies. Barsky was designated as CEO in early 2010. He was supposed to take over TNK-BP by early 2011, after an extensive training program with BP in London and at BP's North Sea headquarters in Aberdeen Scotland, Houston in the US, and Canada.[26] Of course, by the summer of 2011, Mr. Barsky had still not taken his post.

The reason for the delay was the reluctance by the shareholders, most likely BP, to accept an independent manager and an inability to come to an agreement on his contract.[27] Despite his extensive training with BP, Mr. Barsky remembered who his patrons were. But then things started to get rough.

The oil spill in the Gulf of Mexico had been a major disaster for BP. It cost then BP CEO Tony Hayward his job. The problem was that he was replaced by the former head of TNK-BP, Robert Dudley, who, after many years, thought he knew how to do business in Russia. The reality was that he didn't.

To restore BP's fortunes, Mr. Dudley came up with a $16 billion megadeal. He proposed to partner with the state-owned Russian company Rosneft. Rosneft contained the assets of the defunct formerly private oil company Yukos. Its former CEO, Mikhail Khodorkovsky, was tried and thrown in prison. In 2011, he was retried in a second judicial farce and given another term.

---

[25] Catherine Belton, Neil Buckley and Ed Crooks, "Showdown in Moscow for BP and investors" *Financial Times*, www.ft.com, June 12, 2008.

[26] Ed Crooks, "Barsky polishes his skills as an oilman at BP's finishing school," *Financial Times*, www.ft.com, February 8, 2010.

[27] Sylvia Pfeifer, "Barsky calls for change at TNK-BP," *Financial Times*, www.ft.com, July 3, 2011.

Rosneft had the rights to vast reserves in the Russian Arctic Ocean. BP has the technology to exploit those reserves. So, to consummate the deal, Dudley agreed to a share swap. All seemed to be going smoothly. Dudley had the Prime Minister, Vladimir Putin, and his powerful protégé, Igor Sechin, then Chairman of Rosneft, on board. Since his relationships were with two of the most powerful men in Russia, he did not think that he needed permission from anyone else, but he did. [28]

He ignored his agreement with his existing partners. According to the TNK-BP agreement, BP could do business in Russia only through TNK-BP. The share swap with Rosneft required AAR's approval. It wasn't forthcoming. The agreement was subject to arbitration in Sweden.

This "do not compete" provision is common in these international agreements. Most contracts written by Western lawyers have near endless pages of boiler plate. These specify things like choice of law and procedures for settling disputes. CEOs, investors, and the lawyers who draft these documents believe that they are enforceable, and they are, just not in the way that the drafters intend. They are enforceable against the Western partner, but generally not against partners in emerging markets, especially in China and Russia.

Most developed countries' legal systems recognize both arbitration awards and judgments from foreign courts. Since the investor from the developed country usually has most of its assets in a developed country, it will be subject to that jurisdiction. So the award has a high probability of being enforced. On the other hand, attempting to enforce an award in emerging markets is basically impossible. The honesty and power of courts in emerging markets varies widely. For example, some courts in Shanghai may render a Western litigant a favorable, unbiased judgment, but collecting on that judgment is probably impossible because the power of the Shanghai court does not readily extend to other provinces or other government entities. Judgments are often either simply ignored or contradicted by other courts or departments.

The Swedish arbitration panel issued a decision in favor of TNK-BP's Russian partners and enjoined the Rosneft BP share swap. BP was stuck. Even though the decision may not have been enforceable in Russia, it was enforceable against BP. Dudley, by trusting in his high-level contacts, had created a disaster. Not only had he upset his Russian partners by trying to do a deal behind their backs, he had infuriated Prime Minister Putin and Chairman Sechin, who

---

[28] "BP and Rosneft: BP's Russian deal is not yet sunk." *The Economist*, May 17, 2011.

had been assured by Dudley that the deal was possible. He even laid the groundwork for a potential $10 billion lawsuit by the Russian Partners against BP for violation of the shareholder agreement. After all the problems, Dudley would probably have preferred to deal with another oil spill. At least the Gulf oil spill ended in time. His Russian problems never do.

In contrast to the Vodafone experience in India, BP's venture in Russia has been exceptionally profitable. Still, the question remains: for how long? Vodafone may not be making any money, but at least it has a large and growing presence in the market that they are sure belongs to them. BP has plenty of income from TNK-BP, but they can never be sure when it will be stopped by a knock on the door from the Russian tax police.

Indirect Investment in Russia

The Russian stock markets are the smallest of the BRICs and do not even get into the top ten. By market capitalization, they rate somewhere below the Korea Exchange.[29] Russia has two main stock exchanges: the Russian Trading System (RTS) and the larger Moscow Interbank Currency Exchange (MICEX). They both have their own indexes. The two main ones are the dollar-denominated RTS and the ruble-denominated MICEX Index.

Like other BRICs, the Russian market is heavily concentrated in a few state-owned companies. In Russia, about 45% of the market is dominated by five companies. They include Gazprom, the world's largest gas producer, Sberbank, the largest Russian bank, Rosneft, Lukoil, and Norilsk. Gazprom, Sberbank, and Rosneft are all majority owned by the state and make up over 35% of the market. The domination of Russia by a few companies is slightly less than in Brazil, where the top five companies make up 48% of the market, but far more than in China, where the top five make up 27% of the market. India comes in last with 23%. In contrast, in the United States the top 5 companies make up less than 9% of the market.[30] Also, like other BRICs and most emerging markets, the Russian stock markets are dominated by commodities and financial companies. The top five in the US include Exxon/Mobile, Apple, Microsoft, Berkshire Hathaway, and Walmart.

With a concentration in oil, gas, nickel, and other commodities, the Russian market does well when, as in 2008 and 2011, there are booms in commodities. So if you get the timing right, you can do very well in the Russian

---

[29] Wikipedia, "List of stock exchanges," http://en.wikipedia.org/wiki/List_of_stock_exchanges

[30] Valentina Romei and Barney Jopson, "Chart of the week: BRIC stock market concentration," *Financial Times*, www.ft.com, January 4, 2011.

market. If you get it wrong, you can be wiped out. In the 2008 crash, the Russian market lost 73% of its value as oil went from $150 a barrel to $40.[31] That compares to a loss for the S&P of 53%.

Emerging markets can be very volatile, but Russia especially stands out. In developed countries, there are many long-term institutional investors, like pension funds. The US also has a large number of retail investors. In Russia, investors are either local banks or foreign hedge funds that have a notoriously short-term view. Also, like China, most of the shares are held by the government. Only 27% of the shares are owned by the public.

The volatility is even seasonal. "Over the last 15 years, the Russian stock market has sold off every year except for two around the May bank holiday break [early May]."[32] So, the appropriate strategy would be to invest in an ETF around September 1 and sell by May 1. The causes for these seasonal fluctuations are a warning for investors who believe in sustained emerging market growth. They occur mostly in the first quarter because of new allocations to emerging market funds, new money released from Russia's pension fund in late March, and the remainder of the previous year's federal budget transfers made in December that hits the market in January. [33] Of course, as a commodity-sensitive market, Russia is very prone to external issues, specifically endemic disruptions in the oil market.

Again, ETFs are perhaps the only way to invest in Russia. Corporate governance is, shall we say, lacking. According to an American diplomatic cable released as part of the Wikileaks trove, Gazprom is "badly organized, politically driven and corrupt," and "Gazprom is not a competitive global firm."[34] It took two full years for an international accounting firm to get a proper grasp of its activities. Firms in emerging markets have an enormous fondness for subsidiaries. These can either act to help a family pyramid control or hide payoffs. In 2007, for example, Gazprom had an 18% increase in expenses for the purchase of oil and gas. Most of this went to different intermediaries.[35]

---

[31] Courtney Weaver, "Russian equities: shock value," *Financial Times*, www.ft.com, August 9, 2011.

[32] Beyound BRICs, "Russian equities: Profiting from seasonality," *Financial Times*, www.ft.com, May 27, 2011.

[33] Ibid.

[34] http://gulftoday.ae/portal/fd77160b-7c82-4037-808d-bf05581228c6.as

[35] Catherine Belton, "Gazprom hurt by costs," *Financial Times*, www.ft.com, December 6, 2007.

The rot is prevalent throughout Russian companies. According to a survey conducted by PricewaterhouseCoopers (PwC) of 5,400 companies, including 125 leading companies in Russia, insiders were responsible for 38% of economic crimes, and the number keeps rising.[36] The average cost of a theft to the companies was $12.8 million, which is five times the global average.

It would seem fairly obvious that managers who are on the take, sometimes on a truly heroic scale, are not likely to be totally forthcoming about the true nature of their profits. Nevertheless, most Western analysts cannot give up their developed market tools. It is quite common to read about price earnings ratio, price to book, quantitative analysis, and many other concepts applied to emerging market companies without a thought given to whether they might be totally useless because people are simply lying. There is no doubt that Russia is an extreme case, but it is hardly unique among developing countries.

Like anywhere, information has value. It is disclosed for two reasons. Someone pays for it or the law, an enforced law, requires it. In Russia, laws, what little there are, are often not enforced. The security services charged with enforcement are deeply corrupt. Everyone from the traffic police, known generally as werewolves, on up to deputy prime ministers are all on the take. There are huge economic incentives for companies to avoid providing accurate, complete, and timely information. These profits can assure that there is basically no enforcement of information disclosure laws. So the quality of information is abysmal.

But the Russians are trying. At least they have learned from the Chinese that appearances do matter. In January 2011, the Russian Duma finally passed a law penalizing insider trading. It had been blocked by lobbyists for over a decade. The law does provide a prison sentence of up to six years, but its fines, up to $33,000, are hardly high enough to deter anyone other than a retail trader, someone unlikely to have insider information. Even if there was an effort to enforce the law, proving a case is difficult, even in the US.[37]

The law is at least a start. But there is a long way to go. For example, one of the few success stories in Russia has been food. The brightest star is Wimm-Bill-Dann. This company was started in Russia in the early 1990s. As a local company, it was able to survive the debt crisis of 1998 when the

---

[36] Anna Smolchenko, "PwC Says Employee Thieving is on the Rise," *The Moscow Times,* www.themoscowtimes.com/business/article/pwc-says-employee-thieving-is-on-the-rise/193557.html, October 18, 2007.

[37] Isabel Gorst, "Russia: no more insider trading?" *Financial Times,* www.ft.com, January 27, 2011.

ruble plummeted and most of the company's Western competitors fled. By establishing good relations with dairy farms and adopting Western management, it has become one of Europe's biggest dairy products companies. It produces yogurt, milk, flavored milk, fruit juices, and other soft drinks.

A successful company in a growing market, it attracted the attention of the American soft drink giant PepsiCo. On December 2, 2010, PepsiCo agreed to buy 66% of the company. Wimm-Bill-Dann is listed in Russia, but it also has been listed on the US stock exchange since 2002. Many of the shares that PepsiCo bought were therefore listed in the US and subject to US jurisdiction. That did not stop insiders from buying up all the shares before the announcement.[38]

The purchase caught the attention of the American securities watchdog, the SEC, who filed a complaint. Apparently, the Russian securities authorities did not see anything wrong with the transaction, because they denied all of the allegations. No doubt the profits are presently in accounts in Cyprus, far beyond the reach of American authorities, so the probability of a legal disincentive is remote. So, despite the new law, insider trading in Russia will continue.

Even with the legal problems, trading in Russia has some very severe drawbacks. In the US, television and financial news sources are filled with stories about complicated hedging strategies used by sophisticated investors. It would appear that hedge funds happily use these strategies around the globe, 24/7. They can't. Certain simple risk management tools, like shorting a stock, are unavailable in Russia. Current legislation does not specifically cover a legal relationship for securities lending. Other concepts from Russian law are often used to short stocks, but the restrictions make the process difficult.[39]

Although you cannot short shares in the Russian market, you can short shares of Russian companies listed on US exchanges (also known as American Depositary Receipts, or ADRs) or Russian ETFs. The problem with trying to short ADRs or ETFs of emerging markets is finding them. For example, in Chapter 3, I discussed the information issues associated with a Chinese company called Sino-Forest. When these issues came to light, investors in the US and Canada tried to short Sino-Forest and other Chinese companies, but they couldn't find enough stocks to short. The supply of owners willing to lend their stocks or ETFs simply does not meet the demand.

---

[38] Ibid.

[39] Russia, *Securities Lending Times,* www.securitieslendingtimes.com/countryfocus/country.php?country_id=23, July 25 2011.

The central problem with indirect investing is that there has to be a strong nexus between the investor and the investment. The investor is investing money, often "hard" (or what used to be hard) currency in exchange for a piece of paper. The only protection that the investor has that the piece of paper is worth anything is the law. In India, the law does exist, although occasionally the enforcement is lackluster. In China, the law doesn't exist, but at least the Chinese feel that it is in the country's best economic interest to market that it does. In Russia, the reality is that neither the business community nor the government really cares all that much. For short-term investments, during times of increasing commodities prices, Russia might be a good bet. Otherwise, without accurate, timely, and complete information or strong property laws, all bets are off.

Direct Investment in Russia

The problems faced by BP are hardly unique. The Swedish company IKEA is the world's biggest home-furnishings retailer. It has been investing in Russia for the past 10 years. Over that period, it has invested over $4 billion. Its growth in Russia has been spectacular, with rates of over 20% a year since it started.

That does not mean that IKEA has not had problems. It has opened 14 megamalls, but only two opened on time and without any problems.[40] It takes about 300 permits to construct the malls, which leaves plenty of room for bribes. Over the years, IKEA has used just about every means imaginable to do business in Russia. Instead of bribes, it has given large sums of money to charity funds. It built bridges and pledged money to children's sports. Often it is required to donate to "voluntary funds" for the development of the location's infrastructure. It operated on generators when the permit to hook up to the local grid was refused. It is involved in endless lawsuits.

The cost of the bribes to get the permits is not insignificant. The "kickback to officials for getting the right documents could reach 30 percent of the construction costs, and 20 percent to 30 percent for connection to the electrical grid."[41] No money changes hands. Usually these bribes are channeled through local firms designated by the authorities. It has even been alleged that IKEA was involved in knowingly providing bribes. Since the economic

---

[40] Rinat Sagdiyev and Anastasia Popova, "IKEA Masters Rules of Russian Business," *The Moscow Times*, www.themoscowtimes.com/business/article/ikea-masters-rules-of-russian-business/405948.html, May 14, 2010.

[41] Ibid.

incentive of the rentiers bureaucrats responsible for the projects is only to increase the rent, the deals are often broken. One of the few deals that did go through without problems occurred because the co-owner was a former agriculture minister and State Duma deputy.

Still, after 10 years, IKEA stopped. In March 2011, it announced that it had frozen Russian expansion until permits were granted for two outlets in the central cities of Samara and Ufa. At some point, complying with unwritten rules becomes impossible, if not dangerous.

William Browder was one of the first Western investors in Russia. He arrived in 1996. He built his company, Hermitage Capital, from a $25 million fund into a $4 billion fund, one of the largest foreign investors in Russia. He also thought he knew the rules. He assumed that one of the rules was to curry favor with those in power. According to *The Economist*, when "Vladimir Putin became Russia's president, Mr. Browder has been among his most vocal cheerleaders, regularly assailing *The Economist* and others for their more skeptical stance."[42]

When Putin arranged for the theft of Yukos from Mikhail Khodorkovsky, Browder wasn't sympathetic. He did not view it as an extrajudicial example of a violation of property rights to further political revenge. On the contrary, he maintained that Khodorkovsky had it coming. Browder believed that his unstinting promotion of Russia should reap large rewards. He assumed that the rules were different for the powerful and that they did not apply to him. He was wrong, and it cost his lawyer his life.

Browder felt that he was in a position to criticize the corporate governance of some of his largest investments, including Gazprom. As a result of some of his allegations, his visa was denied in 2005. Shocked, he appealed directly to President Medvedev, and then to an aide to Prime Minister Putin at the Economic Forum in Davos. Mr. Medvedev told him he would see what he could do.[43]

What he did resulted in a call from Lt. Col. Artem Kuznetsov of the Department of Tax Crime of the Interior Ministry, who told him, "The sooner we meet and you provide what is necessary, the sooner your problems will disappear." Apparently Mr. Browder did not supply what was necessary, so

---

[42] "An enemy of the people: The sad fate of a loyal Putinista," *The Economist*, www.economist.com/node/5661601?subjectid=349002&story_id=E1_VGGTGDT, March 23, 2006.

[43] Clifford J. Levy, "An Investment Gets Trapped in Kremlin's Vise," *The New York Times*, www.nytimes.com/2008/07/24/world/europe/24kremlin.html?_r=1&hp=&pagewanted=all, July 24, 2008.

Col. Kuznetsov took it. He raided the Moscow offices of Hermitage Capital in June 2007. A few weeks later the documents found in the raid were used to transfer ownership of some of Hermitage's holding companies and drain them of cash. Fortunately, after his visa was cancelled, Browder got the message. He either sold most of most of his Russian assets or moved them offshore. The raiders did not go away empty handed. They were able to change the balance sheets of the Hermitage companies to show losses instead of profits. They filed for a tax refund and extracted $230 million from the Russian treasury.[44]

His lawyer in Russia, Sergei Magnitsky, was an expert at following trails of fraud through the labyrinth of Russia's courts. He was able to uncover most of the fraud that was involved in the process. Far worse, he also uncovered and exposed the tax fraud. For his troubles, he was arrested on November 14, 2008. A year later, he died in prison at the age of 37 because of a failure to treat a heart condition.

Basically, as these incidents show, direct investment in Russia at the present time is impossible without enormous risks. The Chinese and the Russians have shown only mild interest in fabricating a veil of legal authority in order to accomplish their goals, but that is about it. There are certainly many companies who have made a lot of money in Russia. But you have to have an escape clause, because you will never have warning until the door is broken down.

Masters of the universe, like Robert Dudley and William Browder, feel that the protection of people like Mr. Gaikwad is unimportant to their conquest of foreign lands, but they and any other prospective investors should realize that, without legal protection, the bell tolls for thee.

Russia forms an interesting contrast to both China and India. Like China, its government has scant regard for the law and the law's institutions. Unlike China, the Russian government is not strong enough to replace the law. The Communist Party of China, even after its reforms, has retained a firm control over far more areas of the economy. More important, the Chinese government can control information in ways that Putin can only dream of. The Russian reforms swept away both the iron control of information and the power of the party to discipline its ranks of rent seekers. So Russia's corruption increases faster and is more exposed.

Without institutions, local officials are beyond the control of a central authority. What a central authority brings is an encompassing interest of the

---

[44] Ibid.

welfare of the state and its citizens. The local officials are interested in only getting as much as they possibly can as quickly as possible. A good example is that Chinese officials have successfully removed about $129 billion from the country in the past ten years. The surprise is only that they have not taken more. They are limited only by the Party, which realizes that their power rests on the success of the country as a whole. This means keeping a lid on the more extreme avaricious tendencies of the local cadres and apparatchiks. Parties in Russia are only for convenience and discipline is nonexistent.

The Chinese understand very well the value of their brand. The lure of a well-run system with good infrastructure and inexpensive, passive labor has been part of the success of bringing foreign direct investment to China. Insuring that there is at least the appearance of a well-run, business-friendly country remains exceptionally important to the Chinese government, and it is strong enough to make it happen. The state-run news agency, Xinhua, doesn't take any chances. It is even leasing a 60-foot high (18-meter) by 40-foot (12-meter) wide sign on the north end of Times Square to burnish China's image and build its brands in the US.[45] The Russians do not have the power or even the interest to either make real change or to sweep the dirty linen under the carpet.

Russia still has a powerful military force and a vast arsenal of weapons. It has a deep longing and resentment about the former Soviet Empire and its lost superpower status. Its mineral wealth in a world of expanding demand has given it enough leverage to assert some of its prior clout. But this is the curse of oil. Without the financial pressure, there is no need to reform.

India's government, like Russia's, does not have the power to exercise direct control over the economy. It also does not have sufficient control to stop thefts of epidemic proportions by local and even national officials. But, unlike Russia or China, it does have other means to limit the power of government. It has three very important institutions: the courts, free speech, and democracy. Corruption is often exposed and punished either by the courts or at the ballot box.

While Russia does not have complete control over the media as in China, human rights activists and reporters are constantly being either harassed or killed, such as in the case of Anna Politkovskaya. To say the least, this does have a "chilling" effect. Often the harassment is conducted by corrupt officials that are the targets of investigations. Like China, with few economic or

---

[45] Kristina Cooke, "China news agency leases plum Times Square ad space," *Reuters*, www.reuters.com/article/2011/07/26/industry-us-media-xinhua-timessquare-idUSTRE76P71T20110726, July 26, 2011.

legal disincentives and with the protection of a dominant party, corrupt officials from local cops to cabinet ministers have no reason to stop.

Like China, the Russian elite is doing quite well, and unless there is a popular move, it is doubtful that "managed democracy" will ever allow Russia, the Russian people, or foreign investors to realize the country's vast potential.

Brazil

Brazil is a true cautionary tale for investors in emerging markets. Brazil has been "emerging" for the past 50 years. I remember clearly going to the Brazilian Pavilion at the 1964 New York World's Fair (designed by the staunch Stalinist architect Oscar Niemeyer, one of the creators of Brasilia). The pavilion had a diorama in which a sleek, huge, mechanized vehicle sliced down trees and cut vast swaths through the green hell of the Amazonian forest, while at the same time building roads and bringing civilization to one of the last frontiers.

This ecologically unfriendly view of the future of Brazil did not proceed, at least not in the orderly fashion envisioned, but its vibrant vision did capture the energy of the times. We tend to think of the impressive growth of emerging markets as something that is recent; somehow a byproduct of globalization and the technological revolutions; something that began with China. For three decades, from 1950 through 1980, the most exciting emerging market was Brazil. It grew an average of 7.1% per year in the 1950s, 6.1% per year in the 1960s, and 8.9% per year in the 1970s.[1] During those years, Brazil's growth was only exceeded by Japan, which was growing at 9% per year, and it matched the growth rate of South Korea.

For a country as rich in natural resources as Brazil, such growth is hardly surprising. The country has large deposits of bauxite, gold, iron ore, manganese, nickel, phosphates, platinum, tin, and even some of the rare earth

---

[1] Wikipedia, "Economic history of Brazil," http://en.wikipedia.org/wiki/Economic_history_of_Brazil#Spectacular_growth.2C_1968-73.

elements made famous by the recent Chinese restrictions. Thanks to the recent discovery of oil deposits below a layer of salt in the Atlantic Ocean, Brazil's proven reserves are at least 123 billion barrels. This prize puts Brazil at number 6 of the countries with the largest reserves, just behind Iran.

Besides oil, Brazil has other commodities that, with a growing world population, are becoming even more important by the day. Its land is so fertile that, in some places, farmers manage three harvests a year. It leads the world in the production and export of coffee, soybeans, wheat, rice, corn, sugarcane, cocoa, citrus, and even beef. Much of this output is now feeding the insatiable demand from China.

Brazil has a huge supply of another necessity of life: freshwater. Once plentiful and cheap, fresh water is becoming scarcer by the day because of pollution, poor management, and climate change. Although 70% of the globe is covered in water, only 0.007% of the planet's water is available for use by the world's 6.8 billion people, and much of that is found in Brazil.

To develop these resources in the mid-20th century, Brazil relied on a state-led development model. The centerpiece of this model was an explicit policy of import-substitution industrialization. The government limited certain imports with a system of exchange controls that protected certain industries. Like many governments of the time, Brazil gave special privileges and protection to certain favored industries, including the automotive, cement, steel, aluminum, cellulose, heavy machinery, and chemical. Much of this growth was also financed by foreign debt.

Ironically, the government-development programs were instituted by an anti-communist military régime. Such programs were very similar to government programs used in Russia, and India and still in use in China. Like all government programs, they created two lasting problems. First, they introduced large distortions into the economy. The costs of these distortions eventually became clear with the oil shocks of the 1970s. Second, the rapid growth created by the military governments convinced many Brazilians that the state knew best, at least in regard to economic development. Even the subsequent inflation that lasted for the following two decades did not dissuade the Brazilians from supporting state interference.[2]

The preference or faith in state control is not limited to Brazil. It is quite common in all emerging markets and remains the largest impediment to sustainable growth. The most likely reason for the preference for the

---

[2] "Brazil used to be all promise. Now it is beginning to deliver," *The Economist*, www.economist.com/node/14829485, November 12, 2009.

state's interference in a country's economy is often the assumption, by either the electorate or the citizens, that the government will somehow be fairer in redistributing wealth to large impoverished populations. In countries without institutions, or with weak ones, often the reverse is true. Politicians use the government to enrich themselves and their friends and only pay lip service to equality. The result is that many emerging markets have some of the highest Gini coefficients in the world, while most developed markets, with the notable exception of the United States, have some of the lowest.

The Gini coefficient is a measure of the inequality of the distribution of a nation's wealth. If the value is 0, then all citizens of a given country have the same amount of money. If the value is 1, then one person owns everything. Some of the lowest Gini coefficients are, as one might expect, in Northern Europe. Sweden and Norway have the lowest Gini coefficients in the world, with coefficients of .23 and .25, respectively.[3] Most developing countries have very high Gini coefficients, with Latin America ranking the highest. Brazil has the top number among the BRICs with a .56.[4] China, a nominally communist country, also has a high and rising Gini coefficient at .47.[5] Like China, Russia's Gini has been rising to .42, while India's remains relatively equal at .36.

The end of the Brazilian "economic miracle" of the 1970s and its 8.9% growth is also a cautionary tale for today's investors. Both Europe and the United States experienced economic slowdowns in the mid-1970s. The oil shock quadrupled the price of oil and fueled inflation. By the end of the decade, inflation turned into stagflation.

These recessions were not immediately reflected in the economy of Brazil. Much of the profits from the oil, so-called petrodollars, were recycled to the developing world (emerging markets to investors in 2011). This wall of liquidity created an investment boom. It had another effect. It introduced

---

[3] Wikipedia, "List of countries by income equality," http://en.wikipedia.org/wiki/List_of_countries_by_income_equality.

[4] Ibid.

[5] Chen Jia, "Country's wealth divide past warning level," *China Daily*, www.chinadaily.com.cn/china/2010-05/12/content_9837073.htm, December 5, 2010.

the concept of "decoupling"—where emerging markets began to grow faster than developed ones.[6]

The investment boom eventually turned to bust in 1980–1981, when the money spigots were turned off and many of the loans went bad. Today, we have a very similar set of circumstances. Instead of petrodollars, though, we have stimulus money printed in ever increasing quantities by both the United States and Europe. The difference this time is that China has entered the fray with its massive bank lending.

The result in the 1980s was a "Lost Decade." During this time, economic growth in Brazil stagnated at only 2.9% while inflation rose 100%. In the mid-1980s, it grew to more than 1000% a year, finally reaching a record 5000% in 1993. Personal incomes fell by 6%, while growth from 1990 to 1999 was even worse, at an average of only 1.7% per year.

Brazil did finally tame inflation with the adoption of the Real Plan in 1994. The plan, with its dollar peg, lowered inflationary expectations, but economic growth did not return to above 5% until 2004. The Asian financial crisis in 1997 and the Russian bond default in August 1998, and the associated risk of emerging markets, certainly did not help.

But, of course, all that has supposedly changed. As the saying goes, "This time it is different." Risk in emerging markets is, we are told, a thing of the past, because they have decoupled.

Brazil hardly felt the 2008 recession. While developed countries' economies shrank and stagnated, Brazil's contracted for only two quarters and then re-sumed its growth. The mass of money from the United States, Europe, and now China created a demand for Brazilian commodities that has started a new boom.

From a low of 33,404 in November of 2008, the Brazilian stock market in-dex, the Bovespa, more than doubled to a high of almost 73,000 18 months later. The flood of foreign capital did not just go into the stock market, but to direct investment as well. But things change. Inflation has increased over 7% and the Bovespa recently hit a low of 49,000. Over the past several years, emerging markets were marketed as sure things, engines of sustain-able and constant economic growth. But by the end of the summer of 2011, investors took a 30% loss.

---

[6] Michael Pettis, "Some Predictions For The Rest Of The Decade," *Seeking Alpha,* http://seekingalpha.com/article/290446-some-predictions-for-the-rest-of-the-decade?source=email_authors_alerts, August 29, 2011.

All booms and bubbles that are part of a business cycle end in busts. According to Professor Carmen M. Reinhart of the University of Maryland,[7] busts, preceded by decades-long expansions of credit and borrowing, were followed by lengthy periods of retrenchment that lasted nearly as long. There was one common denominator of all of the severe recessions: a large accumulation of debt.[8] But it is not just a question of debt.

An economy can begin to grow again if the debt is extinguished by either foreclosure or bankruptcy. In each of these situations, the creditor recognizes the loss and any collateral is liquidated so that the market can reach equilibrium. The faster this process takes place, the sooner the economy can bottom and resume growth. The problem is twofold. First, the legal infrastructure does not work efficiently enough to allow the mechanism to proceed. Second, often the law is not sufficient to require sufficient information to realize the extent of the problem in the first place.

Legal Infrastructure

In Russia and China, we saw legal systems that just weren't there. In these systems, there is often no way for debts to be extinguished. The creditors are often state-owned banks. The debts are whittled away either with hidden taxes, like larger spreads between interest and deposit rates, as in the case of China, or inappropriate uses for commodities revenues, as in Russia.

In contrast, Brazil has a legal system but, like India, it just doesn't work. This could be a real problem, especially if Brazil's economy continues to slide. Like the United States before its collapse, Brazil is experiencing a credit bubble. Brazil's new middle class has been on a five-year credit binge that has exceeded even the expansion in other emerging markets. Brazil's credit has expanded 2.4 times the GDP, as compared with 2, 1.6 and 1.2 times for Russia, India, and China, respectively. The consumer debt service burden, which stood at 24% of disposable income in 2010, is now slated to rise to 28% in 2011. Prior to its crash, the "overburdened" United States' consumer debt accounted for 16% of disposable income. The number for China and India is in the single digits.[9] This is all the more incredible, since the av-

---

[7] Sewell Chan, "Bankers Told Recovery May Be Slow," *The New York Times,* www.nytimes.com/2010/08/29/business/economy/29fed.html August 28, 2010.

[8] Ezra Klein, "Don't call it a recession" *The Washington Post,* www.washingtonpost.com/blogs/ezra-klein/post/dont-call-it-a-recession/2011/07/11/gIQAVWlF2I_blog.html

[9] Paul Marshall and Amit Rajpal, "Brazil risks tumbling from boom to bust," *Financial Times,* July 4, 2011.

erage rate of interest on consumer lending has jumped from 41% in 2010 to 47% most recently in May 2011.[10] Delinquencies in Brazil (defaults in excess of 15 days) have begun to rise rapidly, from 7.8% in December 2010 to 9.1% in May 2011. They have risen at 23% in the first five months of 2011, which amounts to an annualized rate of 55%.[11]

Brazil is not alone. Credit issues have spread across the emerging markets and, by 2011, have become very serious. China recently announced plans to bail out the local governments by assuming 2-3 trillion yuan ($308-463 billion).[12] The total amount of bad debts could go much higher because many of these estimates do not include off-balance sheet loans. A recent report suggests that at least 17% of Indian banks' outstanding loan assets could be on the verge of default, and debt ratings for companies are deteriorating at the fastest pace since 2009.[13] Turkey has experienced credit growth of more than 30%.[14] Russia's fifth-largest bank, the Bank of Moscow, racked up at least 150 billion rubles ($5.4 billion) of unsecured bad loans. It recently required a $14 billion rescue.[15]

With large defaults looming, each and every one of these countries needs a system to clear the debts, like good foreclosure laws and bankruptcy systems. They don't exist. Brazil did amend certain laws. For example, it did pass a new law whereby a lender remains the owner of the asset acquired with the loan until the last repayment is made. That helps people avoid trying to collect in Brazil's clogged courts. Even with the changes, Brazil still ranks 132nd in the World Bank's *Doing Business* ranking for closing a business. According to their 2011 report, it takes four years to close a business and the recovery is only 17 cents on the dollar.[16] This is an improvement. Under

---

[10] Ibid.

[11] Ibid.

[12] Benjamin Kang Lim and Kevin Yao, "China to clean up billions worth of local debt," *Reuters*, www.reuters.com/article/2011/05/31/us-china-economy-debt-idUSTRE74U26320110531, May 31 2011.

[13] James Fontanella-Khan, "India banks fear rising bad loans," *Financial Times*, www.ft.com, August 23, 2011.

[14] Michael Patterson, "Banks in BRICs Signaling Credit Crisis With Loans Showing Increasing Risks," *Bloomberg*, www.bloomberg.com/news/2011-07-31/banks-in-brics-signaling-credit-risks-as-bad-loans-curb-growth.html, August 1, 2011.

[15] Ibid.

[16] Doing Business 2011, World Bank, www.doingbusiness.org/data/exploreeconomies/brazil/#closing-a-business

Brazil's old law, a bankruptcy took ten years and creditors only received 2 cents on the dollar.[17]

Russia takes about the same amount of time, but the recovery is a little better at 25 cents.[18] India ranks the lowest. It takes 7 years to close a business and creditors get only 16 cents on the dollar.[19] In contrast, the OECD average for bankruptcy is 1.7 years and returns 69 cents on the dollar.

China, ranked 68, is supposed to be the best of the group. According to the World Bank, it takes 1.7 years to close a business and creditors can expect a return of 36 cents on the dollar.[20] Personally, I find the Chinese data very questionable. I have been studying the Chinese legal system for the past 12 years. During that period, with the exception of GITIC in 1999, I have not read any mention in any report or article about one single bankruptcy. The GITIC case eventually resulted in returns of about 2 cents on the dollar. China did pass a new bankruptcy law in 2008, but again, there has not been any evidence that it is being used. What is reported depends on the business. Private businesses simply close down and the owners abscond with anything they can. State-owned businesses just reschedule their loans, merge, or get bailed out.

It is not just the creditor debtor area of law that has problems. The Brazilian government would not interfere with a contract or send in the tax police as in Russia. It does not necessarily discriminate against foreign capital as in China. Instead, it creates a business environment that simply treats all businesses badly.

In 2010, iPhones in the US were selling for about $300. In Brazil, the same phone cost $1,500. Apple does not have a store in Brazil. The Brazilian government went to Steve Jobs, Apple's CEO, to ask him to open one. He refused. He said that Brazil's "crazy, super-high tax policies" were too much for his company.[21] He was correct. Brazil imposes the heaviest tax burden

---

[17] "Survival of the quickest," *The Economist,* www.economist.com/node/14829533, November 12, 2009.

[18] Doing Business 2011, World Bank, www.doingbusiness.org/data/exploreeconomies/russia/#closing-a-business

[19] Doing Business 2011 World Bank, www.doingbusiness.org/data/exploreeconomies/india/#closing-a-business

[20] Doing Business 2011 World Bank, www.doingbusiness.org/data/exploreeconomies/india/#closing-a-business

[21] Vincent Bevins, "Working to a different beat," *Financial Times,* www.ft.com, December 15, 2010.

of any emerging market. Various populist governments have created a system where a hypothetical medium-sized business in Brazil loses 41% of its profits in payroll taxes.[22]

If there is anything worse than paying the taxes, it is just trying to figure them out. Companies within the OECD spend an average of 199 hours a year determining and paying their tax liability. The average time required in Latin America and the Caribbean is almost double. It takes about 385 hours, which is a major burden, but nothing like in Brazil. In Brazil, the cost to complete the tax filing process is an astounding 2,600 hours, or 13 times the aggravation of filing in developed countries. [23]

China recently passed a new labor law that is supposed to provide better protection for workers. It does, provided the workers work for a foreign-owned firm. Brazil's labor laws have been around for years, and they do protect workers. But the system that has been created could be used as the backdrop for a tale from Charles Dickens. Only India compares for creating a system that is guaranteed to *prevent* job creation. The labor law is set out in 900 articles, some of which are included in the constitution and so would be exceptionally difficult to change. The blueprint for the system originated in the corporatist labor code of Mussolini's Italy.[24]

Like the Indian labor law, it is very difficult to lay people off in Brazil. Terminating a worker's employment without "just cause" can result in a fine of 4% of the total amount the employee has *ever* earned.[25] The defense of "just cause" does not include an incompetent or unproductive employee or bankruptcy of the business. The odds that a business will win a suit filed by an employee are less than 1 in 10.[26] With such favorable odds, it is no wonder that 2.1 million Brazilian employees opened cases against their employers in 2009. Like the cases in India, a lawsuit in Brazil can last for decades.

In 1994, three partners purchased a chain of pharmacies. As soon as the sale was complete, the new owners were taken to court by former employees who claimed back pay for overtime and holidays in the amount of about

---

[22] "Brazil's industrial policy: Dealing with the real: The government feels the manufacturers' pain," *The Economist*, www.economist.com/node/21525439, August 6, 2011.

[23] Vincent Bevins, "Working to a different beat," *Financial Times*, www.ft.com, December 15, 2010.

[24] "Brazil's labour laws: Employer, beware, an archaic labour code penalises businesses and workers alike" *The Economist*, www.economist.com/node/18332906, March 10, 2011.

[25] Ibid.

[26] Vincent Bevins, "Working to a different beat," *Financial Times*, www.ft.com, December 15, 2010.

$570,000. The partners couldn't defend against the claim because they didn't have any evidence. The evidence, which would have proven their case, was the payroll records. They didn't have the payroll records because it was the claimants' responsibility to keep them correctly and they hadn't done their jobs. So the new owners lost their case.[27]

The court froze the business's bank accounts to insure that the judgment would be collected. Without any cash flow, the owners had to close some of the stores, which resulted in 35 layoffs. Seventeen years later, three of the cases were finally settled for about $200,000. One case had not settled because the claimant had died and the heirs, a widow and her son, were fighting over how much to accept.

Like India, Brazil's labor laws have ended up hurting the people they are supposed to protect. The cost of hiring a new employee is equal to the amount of their salary. So in effect the employer is paying double for the same worker. If you hire them as an independent contractor, it brings down the cost to only 25% of their salary.[28] The result is that fewer employees get hired, at least in the organized sector.

As usual, in jurisdictions where the regulations are too burdensome, businesses use various means to work around the law. There is even a word for it: *Jeitinho*, which literally means "knack." It is a Brazilian expression for the way of doing things by circumventing rules through the use of blackmail, family ties, promises, rewards, or money to obtain favors or to get an advantage.[29] Words like Jeitinho exist in every emerging market.

Other businesses simply ignore the law altogether. Brazil's underground economy represents almost 40% of the GDP.[30] Brazil's labor laws also result in low productivity and high job turnover. But the government does not see any problems. According to the labor minister, Carlos Lupi, the laws are "very up-to-date," and he wants firing workers to become still pricier.[31]

---

[27] "Brazil's labour laws: Employer, beware, an archaic labour code penalises businesses and workers alike," *The Economist*, www.economist.com/node/18332906, March 10, 2011.

[28] Vincent Bevins, "Working to a different beat," *Financial Times*, www.ft.com, December 15, 2010.

[29] Wikipedia, "Jeitinho," http://en.wikipedia.org/wiki/Jeitinho.

[30] "Brazil's Underground Economy Equivalent to 27.1 Percent of GDP in '08," *Latin American Herald Tribune*, www.laht.com/article.asp?CategoryId= 14090&ArticleId=334886, September 1, 2011.

[31] "Brazil's labour laws: Employer, beware, an archaic labour code penalises businesses and workers alike," *The Economist*, www.economist.com/node/18332906, March 10, 2011.

Pensions in Brazil are also a major drag on its potential growth. Interestingly enough, there is no retirement age. Retirement is after at least 35 years of contributions for men or 30 years for women. Pensions can be claimed while the employee is still working, so there is no reason to delay payment.[32] Public-sector pensions account for over half of social spending.[33] They benefit only 2.5 million former civil servants, about 1% of the population, who are far better off than the average citizen. Civil servants do not merely retire on full salary; they get, in effect, a pay rise because they stop paying contributions into the system.

There is another problem called the Viagra effect. Widows get up to 70% of their husband's pensions for life. Two out of three men who are separated remarry, while only one out of three separated women find a new husband. Of the separated men, 64% of those over the age of 50 remarry women younger than themselves. In the 60–64 age range, the proportion goes up to 69%, and there is a marked preference for women aged 30 years or younger. The Brazilian pension system assumed that widows would outlive their husbands by a maximum of 15 years, rather than the potential for more than 30 years.[34]

It is not just the laws in Brazil that present a major impediment to sustained economic growth; the courts do as well. Like India, the courts are appallingly slow. It is basically impossible to enforce a contract through the courts in Brazil. The process is so slow that it is used as a delaying tactic to avoid performing contracts. The lack of reasonable legal redress forces businesses to seek alternative methods, which is one of the reasons why Brazil continues to be more of a relationship-based system.

Although Brazil's judges are hardly considered paragons of virtue—69% of respondents said that judges in Brazil lack impartiality, according to a 2009 study[35]—the real problem is procedural. Brazilian courts allow for almost endless appeals. The result is that the Brazilian Supreme Court received over 100,781 cases in 2008 alone. These were new cases that are in addi-

---

[32] "Pensions at a Glance 2011, Retirement-income Systems in OECD and G20 Countries," www.oecd-ilibrary.org/docserver/download/fulltext/8111011ec081.pdf?expires=1314907271&id=id&accname=guest&checksum=B9D056C36548235FDD14B7A315F610FA, March 17, 2011.

[33] "Companies are squeezed between an obstructive government and black-market competitors," *The Economist*, November 12, 2009.

[34] "'Viagra effect' undermining Brazil's pension system: study," *AFP*, www.google.com/hostednews/afp/article/ALeqM5j4kRaee74hsEIN15BUNQ-SrvMYKQ.

[35] "When less is more: Brazil's supreme court," *The Economist*, www.economist.com/node/13707663, May 21, 2009.

tion to its backlog. The right of appeal is in the constitution and so it will likely remain.[36]

The effects can lead to egregious miscarriages of justice. Antonio Pimenta Neves is a journalist who confessed to killing his girlfriend in August 2000. He was sentenced in 2006 to 18 years, but with his appeals he was finally incarcerated in May 2011, more than ten years after the crime, for a reduced sentence of 11 years.[37]

Infrastructure

It is not just the legal infrastructure that makes doing business in Brazil difficult. The physical infrastructure also does not help. Brazil has the world's third-largest road network, but 88% of it is dirt. The lack of all-weather roads can be a real impediment in a country subject to tropical downpours.

The railroad system is not much better. As in many emerging markets, the Brazilian railroads were nationalized. In Brazil's case, this occurred in 1957, when Rede Ferroviária Federal S.A., Federal Railroad Network (RFFSA) was created. During the slowdown in the 1980s, investment in the railroads stopped and the system deteriorated. The state-owned company was finally privatized between 1999–2007.[38] Presently, the Brazilian rail network consists of 12 freight lines, totaling just over 17,400 miles of track. The territory of the United States is a little more than 10% larger than Brazil, but it has 10 times more track.[39] So, over 60% of freight in Brazil goes by road and only 20% by rail, compared with an even split in the United States.[40]

The rail lines that Brazil does have are not always available to everyone. The mining giant, Vale, has its own railway lines, which allow it to get its iron ore from the mine to the ports.[41] It also has interests, along with two large steel

[36] Ibid.

[37] "Journalist Antonio Pimenta Neves was arrested 11 years," *Correio Braziliense*, www.correiobraziliense.com.br/app/noticia/politica-brasil-economia/2011/05/25/internas_polbraeco,253747/jornalista-antonio-pimenta-neves-e-preso-apos-11-anos.shtml, May 25, 2011.

[38] Wikipedia, "RFFSA," http://en.wikipedia.org/wiki/RFFSA

[39] Nelza Oliveira, "Railroads poised to reduce logistical bottlenecks in Brazil," *Infosurhoy.com*, www.infosurhoy.com/cocoon/saii/xhtml/en_GB/features/saii/features/economy/2011/02/22/feature-02, February 22, 2011.

[40] "Brazil has learned to love its commodity sector," *The Economist*, www.economist.com/node/14829525, November 12, 2009.

[41] Ibid.

companies, CSN and Usiminas, in another railway. These railway lines are off limits to their competitors.

The airports are another issue. A further relic of state control, the bureaucracy that runs the airports has created more bottlenecks within Brazil's infrastructure. The bureaucracy is called Infraero. It is still dominated by the Brazilian Air Force, a leftover from years of military rule. Infraero is so inefficient that it has failed to spend even half of its budget for airport upgrades. Of the upgrades it has managed to start, already more than half are behind schedule.[42] This is a real problem, considering that the number of passengers is rising by over 10% per year and most of the main airports are already operating over capacity. Brazil is hosting the 2014 World Cup and the 2016 Summer Olympics. Both will be a challenge, since the nine airport redevelopments projects in Brazil's host cities are behind schedule and construction of the new Olympic Stadium in São Paulo has not even started.[43]

Brazil's seaports are burdened by the same issues. Brazil's ports are the gateways to more than 80% of the goods imported and exported by the country. The economic growth in Brazil between 2003 and 2010 resulted in 200% growth in those imports and exports. But Brazil's ports have not kept up. Brazil's 34 public ports are run by a state bureaucracy, and it hasn't made any investments in infrastructure in 20 years. Parts of the ports are privatized, but the state has created a convoluted bidding system that stifles investment. To ship goods requires 112 different documents. The ports now need an additional infrastructure investment of $42.88 billion real ($25.55 billion USD). According to some studies, at the current rate of growth, the ports could collapse by 2013.[44]

The failure to build sufficient infrastructure and the dysfunctional nature of the government bureaucracy, coupled with the problems of the legal infrastructure, are a continuing impediment to the realization of Brazil's potential. According to the World Bank's Growth Commission, to maintain growth, a developing country should invest around 25% of its GDP, of which 7% should be invested in infrastructure. Brazil's investment level is

---

[42] "Dilma Rousseff takes over a booming economy—and rising inflation and interest rates, lack of investment in infrastructure and a fiscally incontinent legislature," *The Economist,* www.economist.com/node/17797502, December 29, 2010.

[43] "Airports and stadiums are behind schedule," *The Economist,* www.economist.com/node/18651344, May 5, 2011.

[44] Nelza Oliveira, "Brazil: Ports operating at their limit," *Infosurhoy.com,* www.infosurhoy.com/cocoon/saii/xhtml/en_GB/features/saii/features/main/2011/02/08/feature-03, August 2, 2011.

getting better at about 20%, but in 2007, Brazil invested just .1% of GDP on transport.[45] The cost of the unequal pension system and the need to spend government money to alleviate poverty doesn't leave room for much else in the budget. The refusal to privatize parts of the infrastructure, like the ports and the airports, makes the situation worse.

Indirect Investment in Brazil

The Brazilian stock exchange in some ways is the most sophisticated and best run of all of the emerging markets. Brazil's stock exchange (Bovespa) and the Brazilian Mercantile and Futures Exchange (Bolsa de Mercadorias e Futuros—BM&F) merged in May 2008. The new entity, BM&FBovespa (still commonly referred to as Bovespa) is the largest market in Latin America in terms of market capitalization and the tenth largest in the world.[46]

For an emerging market, the Bovespa offers more liquidity and a sophisticated platform that attracts large investment firms. It is the first exchange in Latin America to have an algorithmic trading system that would make complex trading strategies used by quant funds possible. Still, like other emerging markets, only 6% of trades are automated, as compared with nearly 70% for the Nasdaq Stock Market and the New York Stock Exchange.[47]

In recent years, the Bovespa has also made major improvements in corporate governance. The rules were changed in 2002 to require greater protection for minority shareholders. There are almost six hundred companies listed on the Bovespa, but they all do not have the same levels of corporate governance.

The Bovespa is divided into segments depending on whether the companies adhere to higher standards of corporate governance. This system started with the creation of the Novo Mercado (New Market) segment in December 2000. There are 105 companies that are listed on the Novo Mercado, but only 13 have reached level 2, the highest level. To be included at this level, the companies have to have at least five board members, of which 20% must be independent. Firms also must use either the US GAAP accounting standards or the international IFRS standards. They also must accept arbi-

---

[45] "Brazil has learned to love its commodity sector," *The Economist,* www.economist.com/node/14829525, November 12, 2009.

[46] Wikipedia, "List of stock exchanges," http://en.wikipedia.org/wiki/List_of_stock_exchanges.

[47] Kenneth Rapoza, "'Quant' Funds Test Brazilian Market," *Wall Street Journal,* March 16, 2010.

tration rules provided by BM&FBovespa, which is good because an investor does not want to end up in a Brazilian court.

Although these requirements are commendable, they are a stark reminder of the gaps in corporate governance for securities from emerging markets. For example, there are 2,815 companies listed on the NASDAQ exchange, and all of them must have a majority of independent directors. There are also strict rules for compensation and audit committees. US equities must further comply with the stringent requirements of Sarbanes–Oxley and the rules of the SEC. These rules and regulations are laws and can have punishments mandated by law, including fines, suspension from the securities industry, and jail time. The rules of the Bovespa, like the rules in India and Hong Kong, are determined by contract, where the worst punishment is limited to delisting.

Like other emerging market exchanges, the Bovespa is highly concentrated among a few large companies. In Brazil, 48% of the stock exchange is made up of only five companies. It is even slightly worse than Russia, where the top five companies make up about 45% of the market. The top five in China account for 28%. The best is India, where the top five make up 23%. That's still large when compared to the United States, where it's just 9%.[48] Also, like Russia and all other emerging markets, the market is concentrated in commodities, usually oil, and financial stocks, usually banks. In Brazil's case, the top two companies are Petrobras, the state-owned oil company, and Vale, the mining giant, which together account for 30% of the market. Next is Brazil's largest private bank, Itau Unibanco.

Brazil has its share of insider trading and market manipulation. This is especially true with mergers and acquisitions, where information about the deal commonly leaks. Stocks involved in deals often see large rises in their share price or heavy volume prior to the announcement of the deal. Brazil does have a watchdog, the Comissão de Valores Mobiliários, or CVM, which has been around since 1976. Insider trading has been prohibited for 30 years, but it was only in the last decade that it became a criminal offense. So far, no one has been put in jail.[49]

The CVM has shown a willingness to prosecute insider trading, but its resources are limited. Its staff is limited to only 450. The agency investigates

---

[48] Valentina Romei and Barney Jopson, "Chart of the week: Bric stock market concentration," *Financial Times,* http://blogs.ft.com, January 4, 2011.

[49] Telma Marotto and Paulo Winterstein, "Insider Trading Infects Brazil Stocks as Almost All Deals Leak," *Bloomberg,* www.bloomberg.com/apps/news?pid=newsarchive&sid=alLE2VkNibWw, July 10, 2007.

only about 10 cases at any one time, and most cases the agency evaluates are dropped because of a lack of proof. As you would expect in Brazil, the decisions of the CVM are subject to appeals to the Appeals Council of the Financial System, which overturns a third of the rulings.

The most egregious miscarriage of justice was the result of the appeals process. Financier and speculator Naji Nahas was fined $11.7 million in 1994 for manipulating stock prices and causing the market to collapse. In 1997, he was convicted by a federal court and sentenced to 24 years in prison, but he never went to jail. A state court later overturned the conviction, and the decision was upheld by Brazil's Supreme Court in 2005.[50]

Because of the reputation for corruption, the number of individual investors in Brazil has remained small. Although it has risen in recent years, the number of individual investors is only 500,000,[51] or .2% of the population. In its own way, this is an exceptionally important number for foreign investors, who should take heed of what the locals know and they don't.

Like other emerging markets, the best way for indirect investors to participate is through ETFs, but many of the same qualifications apply. A small cap fund may only represent small family-owned businesses with scant regard for minority—especially foreign—shareholders. At the time of this writing, there were 10 ETFs that concerned different asset classes in Brazil. With the exception of the iShares MSCI Brazil Index Fund and the WisdomTree Dreyfus Brazilian Real Fund, the others are quite small. Any ETF portfolio should probably only include shares that are listed on the Novo Mercado at level 2.

Any index fund for Brazil is going to reflect the components of the index, which for the Bovespa are going to be concentrated in the five main stocks. Since two of these, Petrobras and Vale, are commodities companies, they will be most influenced by the world price of the commodities rather than by any real strength or weakness of the Brazilian economy. Of course, the Brazilian economy itself, like other Latin American economies, is still based on commodities. Regardless, these two stocks do not represent the strongest aspect of the Brazilian economy, which is agriculture.

Brazil has struggled to broaden the base of its economy to include manufacturing. It has a few success stories, like the aviation firm Embraer. But the

---

[50] Telma Marotto and Paulo Winterstein, "Insider Trading Infects Brazil Stocks as Almost All Deals Leak," *Bloomberg,* July 10, 2007.

[51] "Petrobras Sidebar: Transparency Drives IR," *NYSE Magazine,* www.nysemagazine.com/ petrobrastransparency.

combination of the rotten business environment and recently the strong currency has made the process almost impossible. Any entrepreneur is soon wrapped in red tape, and local manufacturers have to compete with the Chinese, who have the major advantage of cheap credit and currency. So, at least for the foreseeable future, the Brazilian markets are most likely doomed to ride a commodities cycle rather than achieve the promise of sustainable economic growth.

Direct Investment in Brazil

The possibilities of rapid growth from direct investment in an emerging market have only been possible in countries like Russia and China for the past twenty years. Brazil has been the destination for foreign capital for more than a hundred years. Percival Farquhar, an American entrepreneur, became the greatest private investor in Brazil between 1905 and 1918.[52] Then, as now, Farquhar's businesses "lived off government favors." Of course, he was bankrupt by 1913. He rose again only to lose it in the Great Depression.

Not to be outdone, Henry Ford, the founder of Ford Motor Company, created a prefabricated industrial town called Fordlândia (what else?) in the Amazon Rainforest in 1928. The idea was to break Ford's dependence on British Malay rubber for its tires. The problem for Ford was that neither he nor his managers understood the country. The rubber trees were planted too close together and were attacked by local parasites that did not exist in Malaya. The workers did not like American food (hamburgers), American housing, American work schedules (no midday breaks), or American morals (no alcohol or prostitution). The project ended in total disaster and was sold in 1945.

Daniel Keith Ludwig was one of the world's first billionaires. He was number 1 on the *Forbes* list when it was first published in 1982. In 1967, Ludwig, like many before, got the idea that he could produce pulp wood from the fast-growing trees in the Amazon. With the encouragement of the Brazilian government, he purchased about 4 million acres (16,000 km²) of land near the mouth of the Amazon River and started the Jari project. Of course, the bugs devoured the tree, malaria took its toll on the workers, and Ludwig

---

[52] Wikipedia, "Percival Farquhar," http://en.wikipedia.org/wiki/Percival_Farquhar.

eventually turned the project over to a Brazilian consortium in exchange for assumption of the debt.[53]

Modern foreign direct investors include the Canadian beer company Molson, who bought a Brazilian brand, Kaiser, only to sell it to a Mexican firm for a loss. Goldman Sachs has invested in Brazil and gotten out more than once. Its competitor, UBS, bought Pactual, a Brazilian investment bank, and sold it back to its former owner. This establishes a pattern. "Foreign companies arrive in Brazil full of optimism, pay too much for a local firm and then leave when things turn sour, often selling the same company back to a Brazilian firm for a small fraction of what they gave for it."[54] But, of course, this is exactly the pattern one would expect from a relationship-based system.

But none of these problems stopped the private-equity giant, Blackstone, from paying $200 million to take a 40% stake in Pátria Investimentos, a local private-equity firm in September 2010 or JPMorgan Chase's Highbridge hedge fund, the world's largest, from buying a majority stake in Gávea Investimentos, a $6 billion Brazilian fund. Meanwhile, another, Tarpon—a $3.5 billion Brazilian hedge fund partially owned by the endowment of Stanford University—has seen its own shares go up by 143% in one year.[55]

But it is not just private equity. Prospective executives demand minimum pay increases of 20% to 30% to switch jobs. House prices in São Paulo have doubled since 2008,[56] and prime office rents in Rio de Janeiro are now higher than anywhere else in either South or North America, including New York.[57]

"Experience tells us that whenever there is a lot of credit available for emerging markets economies, especially in South America, and if that's coupled with very high commodity prices, the tendency of our economies is to

---

[53] Wikipedia, "Jari project," http://en.wikipedia.org/wiki/Jari_project.

[54] "Foreigners are investing in Brazil, Brazilian companies are going shopping abroad," *The Economist*, www.economist.com/node/14829517, November 12, 2009.

[55] "Alternative investments in Brazil, The buys from Brazil: This year's hot market for private-equity firms and hedge-fund managers," *The Economist*, www.economist.com/node/18178275, February 17, 2011.

[56] Joe Leahy and Samantha Pearson, "Housing boom raises fears of Brazil bubble," *Financial Times*, www.ft.com, May 17 2011.

[57] "Rio or São Paulo? For the first time in decades, Brazil's Marvelous City looks attractive for business," *The Economist*, www.economist.com/node/21528267, September 3, 2011.

spend too much," said IMF Western Hemisphere Director Nicolás Eyzaguirre, a former Chilean finance minister, to the *Financial Times*.[58]

In short, Brazil is once again in the middle of a classic commodities boom that will no doubt be followed by a classic commodities crash. The crash will and probably is happening at the end of 2011. One of the main reasons has to do with China. Like Brazil, China has a major problem with inflation and, like Brazil, may have the same experience.

According to Professor Michael Pettis of Peking University's Guanghua School of Management, what happened in Brazil might be in store for China. "Every single case in history that I have been able to find of countries undergoing a decade or more of 'miracle' levels of growth driven by investment (and there are many) has ended with long periods of extremely low or even negative growth—often referred to as 'lost decades'—which turned out to be far worse than even the most pessimistic forecasts of the few skeptics that existed during the boom period. I see no reason why China, having pursued the most extreme version of this growth model, would somehow find itself immune from the consequences that have afflicted every other case."[59]

So, the cautionary tale of Brazil goes unheeded. The markets and the marketing continue to believe in the prospect of an ever-growing emerging market without a close examination of the present and past problems of those markets and the inefficiencies that prevent them from ultimately achieving what they could. To build the ports and roads necessary to sustain growth, Brazil needs to reform its legal infrastructure, but since laws exist that support the few rather than the many, the reform will take longer than the time it would to build the physical infrastructure.

---

[58] Joe Leahy and Samantha Pearson, "Housing boom raises fears of Brazil bubble," *Financial Times*, May 17, 2011.
[59] Michael Pettis, "Some Predictions For The Rest Of The Decade," *Seeking Alpha*, http://seekingalpha.com/article/290446-some-predictions-for-the-rest-of-the-decade?source=email_authors_alerts, August 29, 2011.

Other Emerging Markets

One major sin committed by Wall Street (besides creating a financial crisis that put millions out of work and causing untold suffering) is creating not only the illusion of constant growth in emerging markets, but also convincing investors and, sadly, many world leaders, that the asset class is filled with markets that are somehow exactly alike.

As we have seen from the review of the BRIC countries, each of these markets has a common relationship-based structure. This ensures a methodology for analysis. It also creates a framework that guarantees they have several things in common with one or two other countries; however, the list of differences far outweighs the similarities. The main thing that Brazil, Russia, India, and China have in common is a history of socialist policies. But even in this regard, there are vast differences. Russia and China tried very hard to wipe out any form of private enterprise. Brazil and India just tried to suffocate private enterprise with bureaucracy. China is at the center of globalization. India is barely a part of it. Russia and Brazil rely heavily on commodities. China and India mostly consume them. India and Brazil are democratic countries. China is not and has absolutely no interest in becoming one.

Each has a legal infrastructure that has encouraged their relationship-based systems in different ways. China and Russia have arbitrary systems that function at the whim of the elite. India and Brazil have created systems where the law creates so many obstacles that it prevents itself from serving its purpose. Each of these systems, depending on global economic conditions, can and does enjoy periods of strong economic growth. But none of these periods creates the necessary basis for sustainable economic growth as advertised by the financial marketing mavens. Yet the sales pitch continues.

It is one pitch in a long line of pitches. Before the BRIC countries, there were the East Asian Tigers. These included Malaysia, Singapore, Thailand, Indonesia, the Philippines, South Korea, Hong Kong, and Taiwan. Prior to the Asian meltdown in 1997, these economies were considered paragons of correct economic management. For example, *The Economist* stated that "The gleaming high-rise buildings that fill the skylines of East Asia's capital cities used to be seen as symbols of the region's economic success. Malaysians boasted about having the world's tallest building; Bangkok bankers joked that the crane had become Thailand's national bird."[1]

The paths of these economies have been very different. Some went on to shed any trace of developing country status. Singapore has one of the highest per capita GDPs in the world. The average Hong Kong resident makes about the same as the average American. The people of Taiwan are better off than people in the United Kingdom. South Korea is ranked just below many of the EU countries and above others.

In contrast, Malaysia never quite made it. It remains in the mid ranks, about the same as many Latin American countries, and at the same level as poorer eastern European economies. Thailand is also stuck just below the world average. The Philippines and Indonesia remain truly poor, at about the same level as India.

Yet despite the vast differences between these economies, they were and to a certain extent still are lumped into the same category as part of the "emerging market" growth story. However, it should be obvious from the subsequent history of the Asian Tigers that they are quite diverse.

Each and every country in the asset class offers the investor quite distinct risks and opportunities. The one thing that remains consistent, except as a matter of degree, is that all these markets are relationship-based systems and all exhibit the four major factors typical of relationship-based systems we discussed in Chapter 2—the dominance of family-owned companies, large underground economies, corruption, and state-owned companies.

---

[1] "Tigers adrift: After three decades of whirlwind growth, many of East Asia's tiger economies are in the doldrums," www.economist.com/node/114999, March 5, 1998.

But Wall Street cannot burden investors with something as complex as actual analysis. You can't discuss the differences between all these economies in a sixty-second spot on CNBC. Thus, Wall Street developed short phrases, such as Asian Tiger economies. Asian Tiger economies of course morphed into BRICs. BRICs expanded into the general concept of Emerging Markets and now we have Frontier Markets. Although the concept has evolved, there is one consistent theme.

Starting with Jim O'Neill and the acronym BRICs in 2001 through Thomas Friedman and *The World Is Flat,* the general idea is that the developed world is somehow declining and that rapid and guaranteed growth is only available in emerging markets. This thesis is so attractive that it has been adopted by almost every commentator, fund manager, financial analyst, money advisor, economist, politician, and even some world leaders. But as we saw with Brazil and the Asian Tigers, it simply is not true. Emerging markets can and do grow, often very quickly. Investments made at the right time can make a lot of money. But this is true for almost any stock in any asset class. Like any investment, the reverse is also true. Investments made at the wrong time in the wrong country can be disastrous.

The O'Neills and the Friedmans of this world are very much alive and well, dishing up the same falsehoods. A recent example appeared on the Dow Jones website, MarketWatch. The article concerned some of the world's smallest micro exchanges, including Cambodia, Mozambique, Laos, Cameroon, the Maldives, Cape Verde, Swaziland, Namibia, Libya, Armenia, Tanzania, and Syria. The author's take was that "these bourses hold the biggest potential for trading in and on the future ... I bet these scrappy markets will beat out anything the developed world has to offer. In fact, in the first days after opening, the Laos exchange zoomed more than 80%."[2] Thankfully, he also noted that "It dropped precipitously afterward." I might point out that the Laotian stock exchange has only two listed companies, both state-owned enterprises.

The commentator's thesis was that many of these countries are sitting on most of the world's commodities and large populations of cheap labor. Since labor is becoming expensive in places like China and since China has a constant growing demand for commodities, these exchanges and the few stocks listed on them have no place to go but up. The whole idea is simply absurd.

---

[2] Thomas Kostigen, "World's smallest stock exchanges can only go up: Commentary: Resource-rich Africa, Asia should be on your radar," *MarketWatch.com,* www.marketwatch.com/story/worlds-smallest-stock-exchanges-can-only-go-up-2011-07-22, July 22, 2011.

The assumption is that the labor force is educated enough to make something and is at the end of an infrastructure that actually allows their labor to be part of the global supply chain. The thesis also assumes that China's demand for commodities will continue and that the commodities can be profitably extracted and exported. Sure, Afghanistan has large amounts of copper, gold, and tin; but its links to the global marketplace do not exist nor can they be built any time soon.

These countries are also exceptionally corrupt. For an investor, especially a foreign investor, there has to be a legal nexus between the investment and the investor in order to make money. First, there have to be sufficient property rights to ensure a corporation has actual title to real assets that cannot be taken away at the whim of a faceless bureaucrat (for example, because his mother-in-law needs a new house). The corporation must also be governed by rules that can be enforced by a reasonably honest court within a time frame not measured in generations. The corporation must also be subject to independent, well-financed regulators with sufficient power to force the management of the corporation to actually tell the truth about its assets. In many of these countries, legal protections simply do not exist and there is no reason to believe they will be created any time soon. This hype is simply the stupid and dangerous idea that emerging markets are just mini Wall Streets, each holding get-rich-quick companies with unlimited potential. The only people getting rich are the financial gurus selling this dreck to an unsuspecting public.

With these caveats in mind, the following will be a brief review of many of the smaller emerging markets. I have arbitrarily limited this analysis to the markets large enough to have individual ETFs. As previously stated, the potential distortion of information makes investing in a specific company difficult. Also, it is unwise to invest in general category ETFs, such as BRIC or general emerging market ETFs. Each country in these categories is vastly different, as are their growth rates. Therefore, these funds will not necessarily capture the potential of a given country. Most likely they will only represent the volatility of all the markets. They will do better than developed markets during bull markets and worse in bear markets. Even less attractive would be ETFs based on derivatives rather than on actually holding the shares of a specific index. The derivatives may either exacerbate the fluctuations or make any profit impossible, except over the short term.

Sector ETFs based in emerging markets should be avoided. An example might be emerging market infrastructure. The emerging market infrastructure story is very attractive, but since most of it is dependent upon government programs in individual countries, the differences are vast. Likewise, it might be best to avoid emerging market ETFs based on commodities. These have names like "emerging market energy fund" or "emerging markets metals." Again, this seems attractive. Who could not be impressed by an ETF that combines the potential of the emerging market growth story with the current fad for commodities?

The problem with this thesis is that it might harvest the worst of both worlds. The price for the commodity has little to do with where it comes from. It will grow (or not) based on global demand or, recently, global liquidity. But it will not grow based on the conditions in emerging markets. If demand is high for a given commodity, it does not mean the investor will necessarily see the value. The fundamentals of the company supplying the commodity may look attractive, but the actual execution is lacking. Many of these companies in emerging markets, especially in oil, are state-owned companies. The probability that these companies will pass along profits to minority foreign investors is slight.

These ETFs could provide good returns, though, if there are other factors driving their momentum. Recently, the massive liquidity provided by the confluence of the United States Federal Reserve's unfortunate QE2 program plus a huge flood of Chinese bank loans has given the combined stories of unlimited commodities demand and emerging market growth legs. As a short-term momentum play, these could work; however, investors should keep an eye on the clock and not expect the promised consistent growth will ever materialize.

Other sector ETFs are problematic as well. Most of these include categories I mentioned earlier. They were designed for developed markets but have been slapped on emerging markets without a thought as to whether these categories might perform differently in a different environment. Examples of these types of funds are country- or region-specific funds in a particular sector, such as the financial, consumer, or technology sector. Another type has to do with the size of the company, as in small cap or mid cap, or another characteristic, such as high yield.

China is an example why these designations are misleading; the financials are all state owned. The intellectual property of a Chinese or Western company with a breakthrough technology would be stolen in about five minutes. Small- or mid-cap companies are family-owned firms with little or no corporate governance and high yield firms could go under at any time with little or no return to bond holders, regardless of a bankruptcy proceeding.

In contrast, country-specific ETFs can capture the growth of a specific market, especially when there is momentum regarding a "story" for a specific country. Since they contain many different shares, they can act as a buffer against distorted information and flaws in a particular country's or firm's corporate governance. Shorting the ETF can also provide opportunities for a market that has diverged from the mean. The problem with this strategy is that borrowing shares of the ETF for a short position may not be possible.

At the time of this writing, there are approximately 15 emerging market country ETFs. To the best of my knowledge, they are all physical as opposed to synthetic ETFs based on derivatives, so the counter party and other risks associated with synthetic ETFs is not a problem. The list includes:

- Asia: South Korea, Taiwan, Singapore, Malaysia, Indonesia, Vietnam, and the Philippines;
- Middle East: Turkey;
- Africa: Egypt and South Africa; and
- North America: Mexico.

I will briefly review these countries.

Asia

There is one thing that has created sort of an exception to the diversity among markets in different countries. Although the rules in each Asian market varies widely, as do their prospects for sustainable growth, they all have one thing in common—China.

China is the 800-pound gorilla in the Asian room. Several of these economies were built on export growth models, especially Japan, South Korea, Taiwan, Singapore, Malaysia, and Thailand. Ten years ago, the major market for all these economies was the United States. A slight recession in the United States could have a major impact on these economies. But this is no longer the case.

The main trading partner for all these countries is now China. While China runs large trade surpluses with the United States, it usually runs large trade deficits with these countries. China has had very rapid growth for the past two decades. Most of the worldwide financial community assumes this growth rate will continue, but nothing lasts forever. As previously mentioned, there are very strong reasons to believe China's growth may slow and its economy may stagnate. If it does, the other Asian economies will not be able to avoid a similar slowdown.

South Korea

South Korea is not really in the emerging market category any more. It has a large and sophisticated market with a market capitalization of about $1.2 trillion. There is generally lots of liquidity and 800 listed shares. While it is hardly in the same league as Hong Kong or Japan, South Korea is in the top 20. There are rules enforced by an active watchdog, but that is not to say South Korea has not shaken off the hallmarks of an emerging market.

Despite its rather advanced development and firmly entrenched democratic institutions, South Korea remains a very relationship-based system. One doesn't generally think of industrial giants—chaebols such as Samsung or Hyundai—as family-owned firms, but they definitely are. Samsung Group accounts for about a fifth of South Korea's total exports.[3] It is, was, and will be controlled by the progeny of the founder, Lee Byung-chull. The present ruler of the firm is Lee Kun-hee. His siblings either run or are married to people who run some of the largest firms in Korea.

Although Mr. Lee has stated he wants to hire the best minds from all over Korea and the world, important positions in the company go to his children. His son, Lee Jae-yong, is President and COO of Samsung Electronics. His eldest daughter, Lee Boo-jin, is the CEO of a luxury hotel chain and President of Samsung Everland, a theme park and resort operator that is "widely seen as the de facto holding company for the conglomerate."[4] The company owns about 62 affiliates. With a pyramid structure and numerous cross-share holdings, one study estimated the Lee family exercises voting rights in affiliates that are 17 times greater than its actual shareholdings.[5]

With power, money, and connections, it is hardly surprising chaebol owners are above the law. Corrupt politicians are available to those who can pay. The difference is that the price is higher. The tax evasion rap mentioned in Chapter 2 was not the first time Lee Kun-hee was in trouble with the law. He has also avoided prosecution for embezzlement and bribery. Prosecutors dropped the charges due to lack of evidence and because the statute of limitations had expired. Of course, the journalists who broke the story

---

[3] http://en.wikipedia.org/wiki/Samsung.

[4] Lee Kun-hee, Wikipedia, http://en.wikipedia.org/wiki/Lee_Kun-hee.

[5] Anna Fifield, "Citizens restless in Republic of Samsung," *Financial Times*, www.ft.com, June 9, 2005.

were indicted.[6] It is hardly surprising that South Korea is sometimes referred to as the Republic of Samsung.

The Korean chaebols, at least the ones that survived the Asian Crisis of 1997, are some of the best run and most competitive businesses in the world. But they are still definitely run for the family, not for other shareholders. This means any corporate transparency or corporate governance that would protect shareholders, especially foreign shareholders, is a matter of the ruling family's whim.

The South Korean system has also ensnared direct investors. Lone Star, the American private equity firm, thought it made a killing. It purchased the troubled Korea Exchange Bank (KEB), Korea's sixth largest bank, from the government in 2003 for $1.2 billion. Lone Star took a big risk buying KEB because no one else wanted in. KEB was insolvent due to South Korea's credit card meltdown, which is now an issue for other emerging markets. Lone Star has been trying to sell its interest in the bank since 2006 without success. It has made two previous attempts to sell the bank, but each attempt ran into all sorts of legal obstacles, including financial regulators and criminal charges. It also ran into difficulties as a result of the public backlash against foreign firms making huge tax-free profits.[7]

Taiwan

Taiwan is sort of the mirror image of Korea. Its stock market is two thirds the size of South Korea's, but has about the same number of companies. Where Korea is dominated by large chaebols, Taiwan has a very diverse number of smaller entrepreneurial companies. For example, there are 40 banks serving a population of just 23 million. The market has grown more fragmented over the years rather than less. The market share of the top three institutions by assets slid from 31% in 1996 to 23% in 2007.[8]

The Financial Supervisory Commission, the local financial watchdog, has only been around since 2004, but unlike many of its fellow Asian watchdogs, it actually does prosecute those involved in insider trading. Still, with the heavy predominance of family-owned companies, transparency and good corporate governance are difficult to enforce.

---

[6] Anna Fifield, "Samsung Chief Cleared in Bribe Scandal," *Financial Times*, www.ft.com, December 14, 2005.

[7] Christian Oliver, "Lone Star struggles with Seoul to shed KEB," *Financial Times*, www.ft.com, August 1, 2011.

[8] Kathrin Hille, "Taiwan's banks feel the heat," *Financial Times*, www.ft.com, July 10, 2007.

Like other emerging markets, the government is heavily involved in the financial sector. It controls a dozen banks, including the six largest. Attempts to streamline and privatize the sector have met with stiff resistance from unions and the public.

The legal system also has its problems. There have been rumors the judiciary is corrupt. These rumors were confirmed by the arrest of three high court judges and a prosecutor for taking bribes to fix the outcome of a high-profile case.[9]

Direct investors have at times had some difficulties with local officials. As a small country, Taiwan is worried its stock market could get hollowed out by foreign buyout firms. The private equity firm Oaktree faced this problem when it tried to buy out Fu Sheng, the world's largest manufacturer of golf club heads. Fu Sheng would have been delisted after the sale. After some delays, the Fu Sheng deal was approved.[10]

Despite the friction, the main issue with Taiwan is its relationship with mainland China. Much of the success of Chinese exporters is not actually due to the Chinese. It is due to Taiwanese-owned businesses that have invested in China. For example, Foxconn is the contract manufacturer for much of the electronics sold under different brands, which may include Apple's iPads and iPods and Nintendo and Microsoft game consoles and laptops. It is a Taiwanese company headquartered in Taipei. The Taiwanese use cheaper Chinese labor. Foxconn alone employs 270,000 people at its factory complex in Shenzhen. But the manufacturing techniques—such as flexible production—that are often credited to the Chinese originate with Taiwanese manufacturers.[11]

However, Taiwanese businessmen often have a much different experience in China than those from developed countries. Because the Chinese know the Taiwanese government treads very softly regarding its relationship with the mainland, the Taiwanese can expect little protection. The result is that these businessmen are often the victims of rapacious government officials. For example, in one case, a Taiwanese businessman found that seven million yuan ($1.01 million) had disappeared from his Bank of China account. "They told

[9] "Corruption in Taiwan: Confirming the Worst Suspicions: The arrest of three senior judges sparks renewed debate over corruption," *The Economist*, www.economist.com/node/16647375, July 22, 2010.

[10] Jessie Ho, "Oaktree allowed to buy Fu Sheng," *Taipei Times*, www.taipeitimes.com/News/biz/archives/2007/07/20/2003370494, July 20, 2007.

[11] "Schumpeter: Bamboo innovation: Beware of judging China's innovation engine by the standards of Silicon Valley," *The Economist*, www.economist.com/node/18648264, May 5, 2011.

me I had never deposited seven million yuan in my account," Peng said. "Apparently, someone inside the bank took the money—even some people from within the bank told me that."[12]

It is not uncommon for Taiwanese businesses to suffer all sorts of expropriations, from real estate to intellectual property. The head of Taiwanese electronics giant Hon Hai Precision Industry Co. Ltd. criticized Warren Buffet's investment in the Chinese battery maker BYD, which Hon Hai sued for intellectual property violations.[13] Taiwanese businessmen are fair game because they know if they complain too loudly, they will be arrested. So, often they just flee and don't return.

Taiwanese direct investment in China is important for two reasons. First, investing in China through Taiwanese businesses substantially lowers the risk for foreign investors. As Chinese, the Taiwanese definitely have the advantage over Westerners doing business in a relationship-based system. Relationships in China can and do go back many generations. Despite the divide between the People's Republic of China and the Republic of China, the cultural and familiar ties are exceptionally effective. Second, the experiences of Taiwanese businessmen in China serves as a warning about what exactly the Chinese bureaucracy can do to businesspeople when they think they can get away with it.

Hong Kong

Like South Korea and Taiwan, Hong Kong cannot exactly be considered an emerging market. Unlike Korea and Taiwan, it is not included in the MSCI Emerging Markets Index. Still, it is, outside China itself, the largest exchange in Asia. It is also intimately tied to companies in China, which is a problem.

The widely derided British Empire did leave two gifts of immeasurable value to many of its former colonies—the English language and a good legal system. The English language, thanks to the United States and the Internet, has become the lingua franca of global trade. Elite education in many former British colonies is always in English. The same is true for many emerging markets that were never colonies at all. High-end London real estate owes part of its stellar value to the promise of high-level exclusive English language education that appeals to billionaires from many countries.

---

[12] Loa Iok-sin, "Government accused of failing investors in China," *Taipei Times*, www.taipeitimes.com/News/taiwan/archives/2011/09/08/2003512753, September 8, 2011.

[13] Annie Huang, "Taiwanese tycoon challenges Buffett's investment," *AP*, www.taipeitimes.com/News/biz/archives/2009/05/05/2003442820, May 5, 2009.

The British legal system has helped the tiny city states of Hong Kong and Singapore to become the global entrepôts they are today. But a legal system is dynamic. It is subject to government whim and the government of Hong Kong is China. The leaders in Beijing, like leaders everywhere, are not keen on limits to their power and the laws of Hong Kong are definitely a limit.

When the Hong Kong exchange was limited to Hong Kong companies only (those registered in Hong Kong and subject to Hong Kong jurisdiction), the value of the excellent Hong Kong legal system was evident. Although heavily controlled and influenced by local tycoons, they had enough sense to keep the corruption under control. These tycoons didn't want to cheat shareholders too much because they realized the value of the brand.

Originally, the only way to invest directly in China was to invest in the so-called red chip companies. These were some of the largest state-owned firms in mainland China and were listed in Hong Kong. The Chinese, unlike the Russians, knew that if they were going to raise large amounts of foreign capital, they would have to be sure that shareholders were treated properly. The Russians were very short sighted and greedy. They didn't care and were happy to steal anything they could. The Chinese were more farsighted, which paid off both for the investors in the red chips and for the China brand. The red chips appreciated rapidly from 2002 to 2007 and shareholders profited handsomely, unlike shareholders of the Russian firm Yukos, who got nothing.

The listing of the red chip firms also yielded fabulous wealth for Hong Kong. Besides being the middleman for Chinese manufacturing firms, it became a financial capital in its own right. Its exchange is listed as the sixth largest in the world, with listings for over 1,448 companies.

But success has come at a price. The Chinese feel it is inevitable that investors will want to invest in China no matter what. The China brand is not as significant as it once was, especially for smaller players. The economic incentives to make a quick fortune are overwhelming. The 2008 crash certainly didn't help because it convinced many Chinese and their leaders of the inevitable domination of their system. So the constraints are coming off. Huge companies, such as the state-owned Chinese banks, are still careful at least to look solvent, but smaller firms, such as Sino Forest, don't really care. The reputation of the Hong Kong market as a safe place to invest is beginning to tarnish.

It is not that the Hong Kong legal watchdogs do not do a good job, but there are limits. One such limit is that one of the stock exchange regulators is not an independent government agency. The Hong Kong Exchange is privately owned and to a large extent self-regulated. This is an enormous conflict of interest. In contrast, the Securities & Futures Commission does do a good job, especially recently. Since 2008, it has actually started to enforce Hong Kong's insider trading rules and has had convictions. It even hired an ex-pat British regulator who "hopes to raise the independence of the regulatory world." He added that "the feeling was that a local is more susceptible to pressure from China."[14]

The real problem with Hong Kong has to do with jurisdiction. The law stops at the border. If a Hong Kong regulator wants something from the mainland, they have no way to get it. For example, Asia Aluminum, Asia's largest manufacturer of aluminum-extruded products, got into trouble after the 2008 crash. On February 13, 2009, it made a tender offer to buy back all its outstanding bonds, which had an aggregate face value of $1.2 billion USD. They offered 27.5 cents on the dollar for the senior bonds and 13 cents on the dollar for junior debt. The holders of the bonds would have none of it. They thought they could do better in court. After all, the company was registered in Hong Kong, although its assets were on the mainland.[15]

The creditors sued in a Hong Kong court to force Asia Aluminum into bankruptcy. On March 16, 2009, a Hong Kong court appointed the corporate restructuring firm Ferrier Hodgson as Asia Aluminum's provisional liquidator after the buyback offer was rejected by bondholders. Ferrier Hodgson got nowhere. It finally had to accept a bid by an unknown company named Golden Concord, whose management included unidentified Asia Aluminum executives. Golden Concord offered 20 cents on the dollar for the senior bonds and only one cent on the dollar for the $800 million worth of junior bonds. The Hong Kong receiver had no choice but to accept the offer.[16]

Malaysia

Alexis de Tocqueville, one of the world's most insightful political commentators, observed that the French Revolution did not occur because the French people were poor. It occurred because people were getting rich and wanted to protect their newly won property rights from the government. This is

---

[14] Henny Sender, "Hong Kong taps Alder for securities regulator," *Financial Times*, www.ft.com, July 29, 2011.

[15] Peter Stein and Laura Santini, "Asia Debt Holders Squirm," *The Wall Street Journal*, www.wsj.com, August 25, 2009.

[16] Ibid.

the problem in Malaysia. As the large, well-educated minorities get richer, they have more of an incentive to challenge an entrenched system.

Since the country gained independence from Britain in 1957, it has been ruled by a governing coalition led by the United Malays National Organization (UMNO). The country is divided along ethnic lines. Of a population of 28 million, the Muslim ethnic Malay population makes up the majority; however, there are large ethnic minorities. Ethnic Chinese make up 23% of the country and have dominated Malay business. Indian minorities make up 7% and are well represented in the professions.

To protect the poorer, less-educated majority, ethnic discrimination was enshrined in the country's 1957 constitution. After riots in 1969, Malays were given additional perks. These include privileged access to public-sector jobs, university places, stock market IPOs for their companies, and government contracts. The result was corruption. The combination of what is basically a single-party state that favors one group, together with a heavily commodities-based economy, has resulted in certain people having connections to the ruling UMNO party.

This is particularly the case with judges. In 1988, the courts ordered UMNO's dissolution. The long serving UMNO prime minster, Dr. Mahathir (1981–2003), took revenge. He had the constitution changed to strip the courts of their independence from government and sacked the head of the Supreme Court and five other senior judges. Since then, the courts have been subject to politicians. Last year, the opposition circulated a video clip of a top lawyer apparently boasting of his ability to fix judicial appointments.[17]

The combination of discrimination and corruption led to one of the largest street protests in years. On July 9, 2011, the independent group known as Bersih—the Malay word for "clean"—organized a street protest of 20,000 people that was met by the police bearing water cannons and tear gas. The present government has promised reform of the electoral laws, the repeal of the hated Internal Security Act, and more press freedom. However, since the ruling party has a high approval rating, the changes are not guaranteed. It will be difficult to revoke the privileges of the Malays and their champion, UMNO. Until such time, Malaysia will not achieve its true potential.

This is sad because there is so much potential. Malaysia ranks a respectable 56 on the Transparency International's corruption index,[18] a rating that is

---

[17] "The winds of change: Could the opposition take power after 51 years?" *The Economist,* www.economist.com/node/11294789 , May 1, 2008.

[18] www.transparency.org/policy_research/surveys_indices/cpi/2010/results.

above Thailand's, but below Taiwan's, which is 33, and Korea's, which is 39. It has also received a reasonably good grade from the World Bank's Doing Business Index. It ranks as having one of the best environments for doing business among the emerging markets. It ranks at 18.[19]

Malaysia is a predominantly Muslim country, but some of the more conservative strains of Islam, such as Wahhabism and Salafi, have not been successful. As a result, Malaysia enjoys a more moderate and tolerant religious climate. This has helped it not only as a destination for Muslims from stricter countries but also as a budding financial capital.

As of 2009, Malaysia ranks third behind Iran and Saudi Arabia in terms of Sharia-compliant banking assets ($86 billion) and third behind Bahrain and Kuwait for the number of Islamic banks (53). Malaysia also issues large amounts of Sharia-compliant securities. Many so-called *sukuk* bonds are issued by Malaysian companies; 58% of the total outstanding corporate bonds are sukuk. Malaysia's total outstanding sukuk—both public and private—amounts to $66 billion or 62% of global outstanding issuance. The financial sector has the advantage of being both broad and varied, with large-scale banking, Islamic fund management, and capital markets activity alongside the conventional financial sector.[20] Malaysia is also rich in commodities, so the global slowdowns, particularly the slowdown in China, will impact its economy.

Thailand

Like Malaysia, Thailand has become a battleground for the winners and losers in rapid growth. Since the military coup in 2006, the fight has been between the older elites, represented by the yellow-shirted nationalists dominated by the Army, and the Bangkok old guard. In opposition are the red-shirted populists led by the party of the former Prime Minister, Thaksin Shinawatra. In this near-civil war, the red shirts have come out on top in the form of Thaksin's younger sister, Yingluck.

But political dissonance is not Thailand's only problem. Like Brazil, there are limits to Thailand's emerging market story. During the 1990s, Thailand might have been able to claim to be a destination for low-cost labor. Prior to 2005, their labor costs were higher than China's. China surpassed them, but it is of little benefit. Their labor costs are more than double those of Vietnam or the Philippines, to say nothing of India or Bangladesh.

Countries such as Korea, with better and more sophisticated institutions and educational systems, have been successful at moving up market, but not Thailand. Because the country has a relationship-based system, its businesses cannot adapt. Joe Studwell is the author of the superb *China Dream.* In his 2008 book, *Asian Godfathers,* he describes the region's business scene as "dominated by old-fashioned, mediocre, sprawling conglomerates, run at the whims of ageing patriarchal owners. These firms' core competence, such as it is, is exploiting their cozy connections with governing elites. Their profits come from rent-seeking: being handed generous state contracts and concessions, or using their sway with officialdom to keep potential competitors out. If they need technology, they buy it from abroad."[21] It's hardly surprising the Bangkok business community would battle rural populists to maintain their advantages.

Thailand remains the second largest economy in South East Asia after Indonesia. Through investments by Toyota and Ford, Thailand has developed a large automobile industry. Manufacturing contributes 43% of the GDP but only employs 14% of the labor force. Thailand has also been successful in developing medical tourism and the largest tourist industry in South East Asia. Still, like other emerging markets, Thailand remains heavily dependent on agriculture, which employs almost half the work force but only contributes 8.4% to the GDP.

The United States is Thailand's largest trading partner, but China is now number two. The Thai economy was hurt by the slowdown in the United States, but China picked up the slack. A slowdown in both China and the United States could not be good. Unlike Malaysia, Thailand is not blessed with a natural resources cushion.

Vietnam

Vietnam and financial marketers like to sell the country as the "new" China. In other words, Vietnam is the quintessential emerging market story, being a poor country like China was twenty years ago and with the same growth potential. Potential investors are supposed to look at Vietnam and assume it will inevitably grow as fast as China. In Hanoi, the government tries to en-

---

[21] "The tigers that lost their roar," *The Economist,* www.economist.com/node/10760174, February 28, 2008.

courage potential multinational corporations to adopt a "China plus one" strategy, sourcing products both in China and Vietnam.[22]

Like China in the 1990s, low wages have certainly helped Vietnam grow. Since the 1990s, per capita has risen tenfold to well over $1,000 per person.[23] Vietnamese low-cost manufacturers have been able to attract a significant share of the footwear and furniture business, much of which used to be in China.

Also like China, Vietnam is still very much a Communist country. The fact that its stock exchange index is called Ho Chi Minh ought to say something. It has tried to mimic the Chinese model of export-based growth, but does not really understand the model very well. They are in good company. Neither did the Chinese.

The Chinese like to believe it was the state and state-owned businesses that were the source of its success. Actually, it was a combination of foreign and local private firms that did the trick. The Chinese are now reversing the process by setting more barriers for both types of firms. Still, there was one thing the Chinese did get right. The various regions of China competed for foreign firms by trying to provide the best infrastructure.

Vietnam has not made sufficient investments in its infrastructures and its bureaucrats stifle private enterprises trying to export. Instead, the government funnels cash to big, state firms that, like their Chinese counterparts, are morphing into large diversified conglomerates without focus or core competencies.

Both Vietnam and China have a special fondness for the Korean chaebols. The idea of keeping the national wealth in a few easily watched and controlled mega firms with the ability to compete globally is exceptionally attractive to party apparatchiks. But they forget the chaebols are family-run firms whose owners have a keen interest in growing the business, not using it as a parking spot for rent-seeking government officials. These firms are run by often corrupt political appointees whose only aptitude is making good party connections. Vietnam ranks at 116 on Transparency International's corruption index. The result is that these large state-owned firms, whether in China, Russia or Vietnam, are going nowhere except toward insolvency.

---

[22] "Vietnam's economy: Plus one country: Cheap labour will not yield gains for ever. But what comes next is unclear," *The Economist*, September 2, 2010.
[23] Ibid.

A good example is the Vietnamese state ship-building firm Vinashin, which raised about $1 billion from international investors in 2007. Its total debts are more than $4 billion and it almost collapsed while expanding into non-core activities. In December of 2010, it failed to make a $60 million payment on a $600 million debt. When the creditors asked for a meeting, the company responded they would be happy to meet, just not at the present time.[24]

Some of the firm's creditors include hedge funds. They are getting impatient and have resorted to a very Western remedy—lawyers. They are trying to exert legal pressure through the courts. Vietnam does have a bankruptcy law that seems to conform to international standards, but law is only a piece of paper. An independent judiciary is something that is simply not in the vocabulary of high officials in any communist country and it is unlikely to rule against a state-owned company. The hedge funds apparently understand their chances of a successful legal solution are slim, a realization which is a little late for some of their investors.

Still, the lack of reform that makes Vietnam a poor investment for indirect investors could help direct investors looking for cheap labor. Lack of sustainable economic growth will mean wages will no doubt remain quite low for the foreseeable future.

Indonesia

If there is one country that deserves to be the object of international investors, it is Indonesia. As far as potential, it far outweighs a country like Russia and has many more possibilities than South Africa if for only one reason—its size. Indonesia is the fourth largest country in the world. Yet with all its population, its economy only ranks at 18, below that of the Netherlands.

Besides a large population, Indonesia is also blessed with many natural resources. It is a large regional producer of oil and natural gas and is comparatively close to the huge Chinese market. In addition to hydrocarbons, it has large reserves of tin, natural gas, nickel, timber, bauxite, copper, fertile land, coal, gold, silver, and other things many Asian countries want, but don't have.

Also, unlike many other emerging markets, Indonesia is actually a democracy that has made an effort at real reform. This process has been far from easy. Since the fall of the dictator Suharto 13 years ago, there have been

---

[24] Ben Bland, "Vinashin: a tough lesson," *Financial Times*, http://blogs.ft.com/beyond-brics/2011/03/07/vinashin-a-lesson-for-investors-and-government/#ixzz1Z5H8Dah8, March 7, 2011.

some questionable moments. However, the election of President Susilo Bambang Yudhoyono wasn't one of them.

President Yudhoyono has instituted some major reforms, including tax, customs, capital market development, and supervision reforms. Good fiscal and monetary policy has created a stable environment and the banking system was overhauled after the 1997 meltdown. Even in 2009, when much of the world was contracting, Indonesia was expanding at over 4%.[25] Even the stock market reached a new all-time high.

But the reforms have not been sufficient to deal with Indonesia's number one problem—corruption. The crony capitalism that was institutionalized under Suharto is difficult to eradicate. Indonesia remains one of the most corrupt countries in the world. It ranks at 110 on Transparency International's corruption index. The only thing good about this low ranking is that it is better than other emerging markets, such as Russia, Vietnam, and the Philippines. Indonesia also does not do well in terms of investment climate. It ranks only 121.

Reforms are never guaranteed. The present trajectory could easily go the other way. In 2010, the effective Corruption Eradication Commission came under attack by senior prosecutors and police and the reform-minded finance minister, Sri Mulyani Indrawati, was removed from office.[26] The wealthy and powerful families who run Indonesia's relationship-based system have learned how to manage its democracy as easily as they learned to manage the dictatorship.

The good news is that in 2011, 28 current and former lawmakers were sentenced to prison for accepting bribes. While this sounds like evidence of corruption, the fact they were arrested at all is major progress for an emerging market.[27]

The other problem for Indonesia is the curse of oil. Indonesia not only has oil, but much of the recent boom has been fueled by coal—to say nothing of gold and all its other natural resources. The pernicious effects of a natural resources bonanza without strong institutions to control it allows for a constant and never-ending gravy train of patronage to an ever-expanding band of government rentiers. An example is that despite this vast natural

---

[25] Anthony Deutsch and Henny Sender, "Indonesia: Regional economic boom," *Financial Times*, www.ft.com, June 7, 2011.

[26] Ibid.

[27] "Indonesia's politics, Corruption everywhere," *The Economist*, www.economist.com/blogs/banyan/2011/09/indonesias-politics, September 2, 2011.

wealth, Indonesia has an infrastructure that is far worse than even Brazil's. According to a government study, there is a need for $150 billion in physical infrastructure, including roads, sea and airports, electricity plants, and bridges by 2014. But Indonesia can only seem to find a third of that in its limited state budget.[28]

For direct and indirect investors, Indonesia certainly does show the promise of an emerging market. Besides all the natural resources, it also has a rising middle class that now numbers about 50 million. But despite a population where the median age is under 30 and literacy rates are close to 90%, Indonesia has lagged behind in manufacturing, another aspect of the curse of oil.

In 2011, the commodities cycle and the problems in China do not bode well for Indonesia's continued growth. Indonesia is definitely a country to watch. As a democracy, it has the potential to solve its problems; but it also has the same potential to stagnate.

The Philippines

In September, 2011, the Manila stock exchange became the best-performing exchange in Asia. Of course it was up only 2.5%, which is more of a statement of the emerging market bubble than the quality of the shares. According to a report by the Asian Corporate Governance Association in 2010, the Philippines had the weakest corporate governance standards of 11 Asian markets.[29]

It is not only that the Philippines has the least developed market in Asia, but that it is getting worse. The report stated the country's absolute score for corporate governance fell 13%. Said the *Financial Times*, "The Philippines clearly went backwards over the past few years under the previous administration. Corruption levels appear to have risen, political interference has increased"[30]

But the Filipinos didn't get the hint. The performance of the Philippines market since 2009 has been excellent. It has risen 150%. According to Val

---

[28] Anthony Deutsch and Henny Sender, "Indonesia: Regional Economic Boom," *Financial Times*, www.ft.com, June 7, 2011.

[29] Roel Landingin, "Corruption and weak rules: not enough to shake investors' faith in the Philippines?" *Financial Times*, http://blogs.ft.com/beyond-brics/2010/09/24/corruption-and-weak-rules-not-enough-to-shake-investors-faith-in-the-philippines/#ixzz1ZA97VSd5, September 24, 2010.

[30] Ibid.

Antonio Suarez, the CEO of the Philippine Stock Exchange Inc., "investors have overwhelmingly given their stamp of approval on the Philippines by rewarding the market now."[31]

Apparently, he has a short memory. In 1999, a stock-rigging scandal almost caused the collapse of the market. The stock, BW Resources, increased 5,000%. An investigation by the chairman of the Securities and Exchange Commission was stopped by then President Joseph Estrada. Allegedly, the biggest shareholder in BW Resources, Dante Tan, was a friend of the president.[32] Of course, the scandal sent prices plummeting and Dante Tan, although charged, was never convicted.[33]

The problems experienced by the Philippine Stock Exchange are hardly surprising. The Philippines, ranked at 134, has one of the worst scores on Transparency International's corruption index. It also scores near the bottom of the World Bank's Doing Business index.

The Philippines is the emerging market poster child for the effects of bad government. The economic situation and growth prospects in the Philippines are so bad that its major export is its people. About a tenth of the population work abroad and remittances make up about 11% of the economy.[34] And yet the stock market performed very well, often because the remittances encouraged consumption, which created the illusion of sustainable growth.

This again is a warning about emerging markets for both direct and indirect investors. There are profits to be made, but time horizons have to be kept short. There is no possibility of sustainable growth and the connection between an investor and his money could be very tenuous.

---

[31] Josh Noble, "Asian markets: Philippines now year's best performer," *Financial Times*, www.ft.com, September 19, 2011.

[32] "The Philippines: Imperfecto," *The Economist*, www.economist.com/node/277539, January 27, 2000.

[33] "Dante Tan cleared of BW mess," *Manila Standard*, www.manilastandardtoday.com/insideNation.htm?f=2010/august/2/nation4.isx&d=2010/august/2, August 2, 2010.

[34] Banyan, "The Philippines and its remittance economy, People, the Philippines' best export," *The Economist*, www.economist.com/blogs/banyan/2010/02/philippines_and_its_remittance_economy, February 9, 2010.

Turkey

Turkey in many ways is one of the real stars among the emerging markets. From March 2009 to November 2010, the iShares MSCI Turkey Index Fund increased over 300%! Currently, though, Turkey may not be the best place to invest. The central bank's unorthodox cut of interest rates to lower capital inflows may backfire and result in higher inflation. Yet, it should still be high on any list of emerging market countries for investors.

It is not that Turkey does not have its share of problems. The constant running sore of the situation with the Kurds is one major issue. But Turkey's democratic system has shown enormous resiliency. It appears it has been successful in finally keeping the military out of politics and in the barracks.

Prime Minister Recep Erdogan, along with his "mildly Islamist" (whatever that means) AKP party, has transformed Turkey. According to one Western diplomat, "What he has accomplished in this country is astonishing."[35] Erdogan has in the past shown some authoritarian tendencies. The police in Turkey have a habit of arresting journalists and even Nobel Laureate authors, but the recent elections helped to curb such behavior. Erdogan and the AKP won the election in 2011 with over 50% of the vote. What they did not win was the right to change the constitution alone.

Turkey has been a candidate for membership in the EU since 2004. The accession process has basically gone nowhere due to hesitation on the part of France and Germany, but the process has still been a roaring success. The process requires the candidate country conform its laws to those of the European Union. Erdogan used this as an excuse to reform Turkey, widening freedom of expression and minority rights while curbing the power of the military. In addition, he made many other reforms possible, thus facilitating business. Turkey ranks at 65 on the Doing Business index, which is below most of Europe and the United States, but far above the BRICs and even Italy and Greece.

The rise of the AKP has also represented a major power shift. Turkey used to be controlled by a more secular clique in Istanbul. The base of the AKP is the entrepreneurial middle class of central Anatolia. It is more socially conservative and religiously observant than its sophisticated city cousins, which has had an effect on corruption.[36]

---

[35] David Gardner, "Turkey: Eyes on a higher prize," *Financial Times*, www.ft.com, June 9, 2011.

[36] Ibid.

One of the earliest election promises of the AKP was to clean up politics as part of their moral religious emphasis. They have done a reasonable job. In 2004, Turkey ranked 77 on the corruption index, tying with Egypt and Morocco. Turkey has risen to 56 to tie with Malaysia, while Morocco has fallen to 85 and Egypt still further to 98. This certainly has made doing business easier and more transparent.

The AKP have also helped streamline the banking system. Ten years ago, there were more than 80 banks. Today, there are about 40, with the top seven banks controlling 80% of the banking sector's assets of about $626 billion. They are stronger, with an average 19% capital adequacy ratio at the end of 2010 and are more profitable, with 16% return on equity for the sector.[37]

The failure to gain EU membership has had one promising effect. Turkey is now looking east, not west. The problem with relationship-based systems is that you need relationships. Turkey is a Muslim country with good diplomatic relations with most of the Muslim countries in the region. Its businesses have good contacts and longstanding experience in these areas. When you do business with a Turkish company as a direct investor, the process is subject to the more developed and reforming legal infrastructure of Turkey. The political instability of the Middle East can be a real nightmare for any company; therefore, it is better to work with a partner who knows the territory. Turkey has always been a bridge between east and west. Its present success has made this an excellent time to take advantage of its connections.

Egypt

As one of the largest countries and markets in the Arab world, Egypt is potentially a high-growth country. Certainly, reforms over the past few years have borne fruit, at least for the well connected. But revolt has changed everything and economic reform will not be easy.

The Middle Eastern countries have the largest proportion of young people in the world—38% of Arabs are under 14.[38] However, this is a detriment rather than an asset because an extremely high proportion of the population is unemployed. The frustrations of jobless young men were no doubt the origins of the Arab Spring. They could challenge entrenched regimes because

---

[37] Lex, "Turkish banks: not for the faint-hearted," *Financial Times*, www.ft.com, June 9, 2011.

[38] "Self-doomed to failure: An unsparing new report by Arab scholars explains why their region lags behind so much of the world," *The Economist*, www.economist.com/node/1213392, July 23, 2009.

they had nothing to lose. But creating jobs in an unstable environment will be harder still.

Many of the jobs in Egypt were provided by the public sector. In 2007, Egypt's civil service was about seven million[39] strong in a country with a population of about 80 million. Much of the country's businesses were successful due to the patronage of the Mubarak regime. Other countries have shown that these connected businesses and the families that control them have remarkable resiliency. Even after a change in regime, they are typically managing to make their peace with or even control incoming politicians.

The new voters have been left out of the loop for so long that they will no doubt want a redivision of the spoils and their newly elected politicians will want to make them happy. Thus, the state may expand, not retreat. Add a little fiscal irresponsibility and there may be a mess.

Egypt may improve in time. If it is fortunate enough to elect the right leaders who can actually build institutions, Egypt could prosper; otherwise it is a country to be avoided.

South Africa

South Africa has recently been designated (or capitalized) by financial marketing departments as the S in BRICS. It certainly has potential. Based on GDP, it ranks at number 26 in the world. Most investors would look at its vast mineral wealth. It has 90% of the world's known platinum reserves, 80% of the world's manganese, 70% of the world's chrome, and 40% of the world's gold, as well as a large amount of coal.

From October of 2008 to July of 2011, the two ETFs for South Africa have doubled. The stock market index has risen 70% over the same period, but it dropped 40% in 2008. The stock market is also the largest in Africa, one of the largest of the emerging markets and one of the most sophisticated. It should be. Unlike some of its emerging market cousins, which have been in existence for less than two decades, the Johannesburg Stock Exchange has been around for more than a century. It has had an insider trading law for many years and actually enforces it.

South Africa also has a number of world-class corporations. For example, SABMiller, founded in 1885, is one of the largest brewers in the world. It sells more than 200 beer brands in over 75 countries. South Africa has 18

---

[39] "Waking from its sleep," *The Economist*, www.economist.com/node/14082930, July 23, 2009.

"African champions" in the Boston Consulting Group's list of 40 fast-growing African companies with global ambitions.[40]

South Africa is best described as a first-world and a third-world country all in one.[41] Over 50% of its citizens live below the poverty line and its GINI coefficient is the second highest in the world. Few of its citizens benefit from the geologic bonanza. Its unemployment rate is officially at 25%, but it could be as high as 40%. Unemployment falls unequally on the black and the young. Over 50% of South African blacks aged 15 to 24 are unemployed.[42] Not a single net job has been added since the end of apartheid.[43]

The manufacturing sector, which has created so much employment in Asia, is quite small in South Africa, at only 13.3%. With high unemployment, labor costs are quite low, but the education system is woefully inadequate and there is a shortage of skilled labor. In addition, the infrastructure is often poor and the currency strong, which deters foreign investment.

Unlike the other BRICs, South Africa has a small home market. It has a population of just 50 million, behind Italy and ahead of South Korea. But like Turkey, it does have something else. It is a country with a reasonably sophisticated legal system and connections across a vast continent that pays scant deference to law. This allows partnerships between western companies with more sophisticated technologies and South African companies that understand the territory. For example, Blue Label Telecoms, which sells pre-paid tokens, has formed relationships with tribal chiefs and popular gospel singers to help sell its products. SABMiller makes cheap beer in Uganda with local ingredients. Caterpillar has teamed up with the South African company Barloworld, and Microsoft with Blueworld, to reach African markets.[44]

The South African combination of local knowledge and contacts together with South African legal protections allows both direct and indirect investors to realize the potential from emerging markets. The vast possibilities of Africa can be exploited and the rewards of these risks kept.

---

[40] "Long walk to innovation: South Africa has been slow to innovate. That may be changing," *The Economist*, www.economist.com/node/21528612, September 10, 2011.

[41] Ibid.

[42] "Jobless growth: The economy is doing nicely—but at least one person in three is out of work," *The Economist*, www.economist.com/node/16248641, June 3, 2010.

[43] "Long walk to innovation: South Africa has been slow to innovate. That may be changing," *The Economist*, www.economist.com/node/21528612, September 10, 2011.

[44] Ibid.

There are two issues, though. First, like many Asian countries, China has overtaken America, Japan, Germany, and Britain to be South Africa's biggest trading partner. South Africa has done very well in the China- and liquidity-fueled commodities boom, but as China slows, that boom will most likely turn to bust. Part of the boom is the gold bubble. South Africa is no longer the world's largest producer. It is fourth behind China, Australia, and the United States. But gold does earn over $62 billion in foreign exchange and is the second largest export after platinum. As the gold bubble deflates, so will this income.

The second problem is the same as in the Arab countries. A large unemployed pool of young men is subject to populist impulses. This is certainly true of South Africa where Julius Malema, the rabble-rousing, racial epithet-spewing leader of the ruling African National Congress's Youth League, talks about nationalizing large parts of the economy and taking over white-owned farms without compensation, a radical solution that has ruined Zimbabwe.

Like Singapore, South Africa is fortunate to have a legacy of British legal infrastructure. If South Africa can capitalize on the protection of property rights yet use its skills as a dragoman between the world and the relationship-based systems of Africa, it will indeed become very successful. If not, it will simply stagnate.

Mexico

Mexico, like other emerging markets, is a prisoner of its geography and history. Its geography has placed it in proximity to an enormous market, which has at different times been either an enormous benefit or a curse. The country has had a series of very poor governments. Most recently, the one-party state, dominated by the Institutional Revolutionary Party (PRI), has given way to a far more competitive democracy. Mexico's relationship with the United States and participation in the North American Free Trade Agreement has given it access to a very large, very rich market. However, it also has given it paralyzing drug wars.

The PRI granted favors that allowed different groups to skim off large parts of the country's wealth. This includes not just monopolists such as Carlos Slim, but certain unions that have done very well.

For example, Mexico's teacher's union, the National Union of Education Workers (SNTE), is the single biggest union (of any sort) in Latin America, with more than 1.2 million members. It is run by Elba Esther Gordillo, known as "La Maestra" ("The Teacher"). Ms. Gordillio has done very well from favors. She owns mansions in Mexico City and California. Her property also includes a private jet and she sports $1,200 shoes and a matching $5,500 purse. Thanks to the lessons taught by Ms. Gordillo, Mexico's education system performs on a par with the schools in Jordan, which is half as rich. No one messes with The Teacher because she controls a million or so votes.[45]

Another sacred cow is Pemex, the state-owned oil company. On March 18 of every year, the country celebrates the 1938 move to nationalize it. They should hold a day of mourning instead. Like other oil-producing countries, the income from oil makes up a large percentage of the government's income (over a third). But like Venezuela, the lack of investment and foreign know-how has resulted in falling production, from about 3.4 million barrels a day in 2004 to just 2.6 million today.

Pemex may not be contributing as much as it did to the Mexican treasury, but it is helping someone else. The real beneficiary of its largess is its union. It has over 140,000 employees, far more than is reasonable or even sane, and they are paid very well.

It was hoped that the end of the PRI's monopoly on power would also lead to reform, but so far this has not been the case. The first non-PRI president, Vicente Fox, attempted a reform agenda that was supposed to include tax reform, labor law reform, and even a new private investment in the oil sector, but nothing was achieved.

Fox's successor, Felipe Calderón, is probably the better politician, but his razor-thin victory in the 2006 presidential election did not give him a sufficient mandate. Also, the President's party does not control the legislature and after 2009, the PRI gained a plurality; thus, getting anything accomplished is difficult.

The result has been stagnation. According to Transparency International's annual corruption perception index, Mexico ranked 58 in 1999 but by 2010 it had fallen to 98. Also in 1999, the World Economic Forum ranked Mexico at 34 on its competitiveness index. In its 2011–2012 ranking, it comes in at 58, just above Turkey.[46]

---

[45] T.W., "Mexico's teachers' union: An expensive handbag fight," *The Economist*, www.economist.com/blogs/americasview/2011/07/mexicos-teachers-union, July 7, 2011.

[46] Adam Thomson, "Mexico: Downward drift," *Financial Times*, www.ft.com, June 29, 2010.

This is a perfect example of one of the central myths of emerging markets. This is the myth of continuing reform. Emerging markets have done very well thanks to reform. It has brought millions out of poverty, but there is no political or economic reason why reform should continue. On the contrary, there are many reasons why it should reverse. As Mancur Olson pointed out, as the pie gets bigger, power players such as Carlos Slim, the SNTE, or the PRI all want larger pieces and they have the power to stop the pie from growing.

Mexico also has another headwind—China. Many other emerging markets have done very well from the boom in China by selling commodities. Not Mexico. China is a direct competitor in terms of Mexico's role as a manufacturing base for the United States. Mexico's share of US imports fell from 11.2% in 2000 to 10.7% in 2006.

Since the bottom of the market in 2009, indirect investors have done rather well in Mexico. The local stock index has outperformed the S&P 500 most of the time. The most likely explanation is that the Mexican exchange has benefitted from the momentum associated with other emerging markets. Momentum and "stories" are both powerful forces. However, the reverse is also true. As with other emerging markets, the Mexican Bolsa can be far more volatile than its developed-market counterparts. As the cycle turns, the market can go a lot lower.

This no doubt will be helped by the usual issues with corporate governance. Mexico shares with other emerging markets the habit of neglecting to prosecute those involved in insider trading. Although insider trading has been outlawed since 1975, no one was formally accused of insider trading until 2002.[47] With the lack of good corporate governance and the distortions from failure to provide accurate and timely information, ETFs are no doubt the best way to invest indirectly in Mexico.

As for direct investors, the relationships between many US citizens of Mexican descent and Mexicans go back generations. For once, investors from the United States have a distinct advantage over investors from other developed markets. The Americans know the territory.

---

[47] Juan J. Cruces and Enrique Kawamura, "Insider Trading and Corporate Governance in Latin America: A Sequential Trade Model Approach," www.udesa.edu.ar/files/Public/Doc/Eco/DOC86.PDF, November 30, 2005.

Frontier Markets

The marketing campaign led by the "Mad Men" of Wall Street has been very successful in selling both the BRIC countries and emerging markets. It has created untold profits for all sorts of investment and financial firms, to say nothing of the quantity of conferences and even academic papers. But to repeat the success, one needs a new product and Wall Street has one.

The new asset class is called Frontier Markets. The idea is to get in on the ground floor of the "new China." Even the venerable *Financial Times* describes these markets as "a lot like emerging markets a generation ago."[48] So these assets are being sold as a chance to get in on the ground floor of a no-lose growth story.

A good example of frontier markets is the MSCI Frontier Emerging Markets Index of 26 countries, which basically includes every market not part of another index. A little more discriminating is the selection of the ever-inventive Goldman Sachs. Imaginatively called the Goldman 11, these countries include South Korea, Mexico, Indonesia, Turkey, the Philippines, Egypt, Vietnam, Pakistan, Nigeria, Bangladesh, and Iran.

Attempting to replicate the success of the BRIC brand are the CIVETS. These include Colombia, Indonesia, Vietnam, Egypt, Turkey, and South Africa. The choice of the civet, a mammal, might be accurate. The civet is known for two things, creating very expensive coffee by ingesting and excreting the coffee bean and possibly being the source of an interspecies virus known as severe acute respiratory syndrome (SARS).

Despite the odd names, there is some truth to the Frontier Market "story." In the last six months of 2010, the MSCI Frontier Markets Index did outperform the emerging markets by gaining 16.5% compared to 12.3%. Of course, this is a rather recent phenomenon. After doing quite well from 2003 to mid-2008, frontier markets collapsed. Like all markets, frontier markets did recover, but until recently they underperformed not only the emerging market index by 27%, but the S&P 500 as well.

In terms of economic growth, these markets are very attractive, with some of the fastest growing economies in the world. Their debt burden is often lower than both emerging and developed markets. Their growth seems generally to have a lower correlation to both emerging and developed markets and at 13 times earnings, their equities seem quite cheap. Besides, they all have growing populations with young cheap labor.

---

[48] Lex, "Frontier markets," *Financial Times*, www.ft.com, December 21 2010.

But the happy talk only goes so far. There is another side to the story. First, other than marketing, the grouping of frontier markets has no purpose. To place countries as different as Kuwait, Argentina, Bangladesh, Kenya, and Estonia in the same group is simply silly. These countries, their markets, economies, and growth prospects have really nothing to do with each other.

Many of the problems for investors in these countries are similar to those in other emerging markets, except on a larger scale. Their legal infrastructures are exceptionally economically inefficient, if they exist at all. Many have high levels of political instability and some are nearly failed states. According to Transparency International's corruption index, some countries in this group, such as Qatar and Estonia, rank fairly high (19 and 26, respectively). However, most do not. Few rank even in the top 100. Countries such as Bangladesh, Nigeria, and the Philippines are all tied at 134.

Like many emerging markets, Frontier Markets are dominated by state-owned and family-owned companies. According to one ranking by the Asian Corporate Governance Association, their corporate governance is rather low. Indonesia and the Philippines ranked at the bottom for Asia, with scores of 40 and 37, respectively. In contrast, Singapore has a score of 67 out of 100.

Their labor forces are young, but sadly their economies are often growing too slowly to provide jobs. Unemployment rates among younger workers are often as high as 40%. Education does not seem to help. According to the IMF, the unemployment rate in Egypt, Jordan, and Tunisia exceeds 15%, even for workers with a tertiary education.

Also, the growth assumptions may be dependent on some potentially short-term effects. For example, the African investment story is based on a belief that Chinese demand will continue. According to recent research at the IMF, the quantitative monetary easing (QE2) in the United States has transferred itself almost completely to emerging markets.

The result is often highly volatile markets. Presently, Chile, Peru, Indonesia, the Philippines, Sri Lanka, Taiwan, and Thailand are all at or near all-time highs. In the past, many of these markets have dropped by enormous amounts. In 2008, Egypt dropped 60%. While this was similar to the S&P 500, its recovery is not. While the S&P 500 was only 17% off its all-time high in early 2011, Egypt is still 36% below its peak. Kuwait has recovered only 4% since 2008 and is still 54% off its all-time high. Saudi Arabia reached its peak in 2006. Even after five years, it is trading at only 35% of its peak.

While the promise is there, it is exceptionally important for investors to make sophisticated distinctions between these markets. Strategies that might be applicable to more developed markets have no use in frontier markets. And as always, new highs should be a signal for caution rather than the promise of greater profits.

Emerging Market Bonds

In the fall of 2010, the United States Federal Reserve started a process of quantitative easing known as QE2. It had and most likely will continue to have many unfortunate and unintended consequences. The idea behind QE2 was that it was supposed to drive US interest rates so low that investors would seek higher yields by investing in riskier assets. In this regard, it did accomplish its goal. With interest rates for US government and corporate bonds at all-time lows, investors went looking for higher yields. No doubt the Federal Reserve thought investors would confine their search to the United States. They were wrong. They didn't. In a globalized world, investors looked everywhere, often in all the wrong places.

Emerging market sovereign debt quite recently seemed to involve quite a bit of risk. After all, investing in debt or fixed income investments is supposed to be a conservative investment without either risk or the volatility of equities. Emerging markets are supposed to involve a great deal of volatility, currency, and political risk. How could they become so respectable? One word—Greece.

In contrast to Greece and may of the other Eurozone basket cases, the balance sheets of many emerging markets look quite strong. While both Italy and Japan have debt to GDP ratios above 100% (almost 200% in the case of Japan), the debts of Brazil, Turkey, Mexico, Poland, and even South Africa are all below 50%. Tony Crescenzi of PIMCO put it very simply, "Investors are asking themselves, 'Would I rather lend money to nations whose debt burden is worsening, or to nations where it is improving?' "[49]

Not only are the balance sheets often stronger, the yields are as well. As of October 2011, the yield for ten-year bonds from Mexico is 6.01% and for Brazil it is 11.61%. Ten-year bonds in the United States are yielding only 2.16% and Japan's ten-year Japan Government Bonds (JGBs) yields only 1.02%.

But what are the risks? First, there is the currency risk. In the past, unstable emerging market economies produced high inflation and volatile currencies. Often, they would borrow in dollars, which caused a crisis if their currencies fell. Today, the situation may be reversed. The credit ratings of many

---

[49] "In a hole: Stagnation, default or inflation await. The only way out is growth," *The Economist*, www.economist.com/node/16397098, June 24, 2010.

emerging markets are good enough to allow them to borrow in their own currencies.

The currency risks have also changed. Much has been written about the undervalued renminbi; it is not alone. *The Economist*'s most recent Big Mac index, a measure of currency valuations according to purchasing power parity, showed that several emerging markets, including Mexico and Indonesia, have substantially undervalued currencies.[50] In contrast, the Brazilian real is the most overvalued currency. So there is potential for both currency gains and losses depending on the country.

Inflation has always been a headache for emerging markets. Governments would often follow unsustainable development and social programs financed by international borrowing and printing money. Again, it appears the situation is reversed, as central banks in developed countries follow extraordinary loose monetary policies to avoid a nasty recession. But appearances can be deceiving. Since the crash, the booming economies of the emerging markets have caused several countries to have rather resilient inflation rates that have so far resisted interest rate hikes. As of October, 2011, India's inflation rate is almost 10%. China's reported rate is 6.1%, although it is likely much higher. Brazil's inflation rate is 7.31%. The rates of all three countries are still rising.

There are other problems as well, including trying to determine the risk. The Greek crisis was certainly exacerbated by dodgy accounting. According to Pierre Cailleteau of Moody's, a rating agency, "the state of public-finance accounting is extremely rudimentary relative to private-sector accounting." Greece is subject to EU rules, has a democratic government, and a free press. Even so, they distorted their numbers. Greece's budget issues were discovered when the newly elected Socialist government revealed a double-digit deficit in October of 2009, a deficit that was almost three times the previous forecast. It wasn't a mistake. The Greek bean counters had been at this game a long time. According to Eurostat, the European Union statistical agency, Greece distorted its numbers to get into the EU in 2001.[51]

Governments make laws, but they do not necessarily have to obey them. Investors always have to remember the agencies that compile statistics are controlled by governments and do not really have to answer to anyone.

---

[50] "The Big Mac index: Currency comparisons, to go," *The Economist*, www.economist.com/blogs/dailychart/2011/07/big-mac-index, July 28, 2011.

[51] Kerin Hope, "History of statistics that failed to add up," *Financial Times*, www.ft.com, September 30, 2011.

Other legal institutions that allow for access to accurate information simply do not exist in many emerging markets, so the optimistic numbers may only give the illusion of solvency. The reality may be quite different.

It is not only information about governments that creates risk in emerging markets. It is the governments themselves. According to a recent study, increased government interference in the economies of developed markets has resulted in less efficient use of resources. For each percentage point increase in the share of GDP devoted to government spending, growth was reduced by 0.12–0.13% a year.[52] Emerging markets such as India, China, and Russia are dominated by government. In all these countries, the government sector is over 50% of the economy. Therefore, the present fiscal situation could change rapidly.

In fact, it is already changing. Due to demand, emerging market corporate and sovereign bonds have been issued at a record pace. They are 10% above 2009, itself a record year. This new debt may cause problems because of the nature of debt itself.

In game theory, a debtor's best move is not to pay back the creditor. Debtors do so for only two reasons, the law and reputation. An enforced law can require a debtor to repay. Without the law, creditors must rely on reputation. If a debtor earns a bad reputation, then they cannot borrow in the future.

The problem with sovereign debt is that governments make the law, so collecting from defaulters like Argentina has been exceptionally difficult. Usually, when a country defaults, the restructuring is basically dictated by the defaulting state. Creditors take the deal, often because there are no alternatives.

Certainly, sovereign debt from emerging markets carries associated risks, but government is government. The debt is issued by a country, which can't really just disappear. In time, most sovereign defaults are worked out. However, such logic is not always convincing. Tom Becket, chief investment officer at PSigma Investment Management, states "I think people are probably giving emerging market governments too much credence in their ability to manage their way through potential financial crises. I would still much rather

---

[52] "The unkindest cuts: Many countries face the difficult choice of upsetting the markets or upsetting their voters," *The Economist*, www.economist.com/node/16397086, June 24, 2010.

invest with high quality emerging market companies and their management than with the politicians of certain emerging market countries." [53]

With such faith and with mounting risks associated with government bonds in developed markets, emerging market countries and corporations were able to issue more debt than ever before. In 2010, they issued $151 billion dollars in dollar-denominated debt, more than in any other year.[54]

China was a preferred destination for yield-seeking investors. In 2010, Chinese companies raised three times more money from bonds as they did from equities. The sales continued to break records this year. Chinese corporate yuan-denominated bond sales totaled over 100 billion yuan ($15.2 billion), up 60% over 2010. Dollar-denominated bonds did even better. Chinese companies also broke records, with sales of $33 billion.[55] Chinese real estate developers alone have sold more than $19 billion in recent years.[56]

Now, many of these bonds are beginning to go bad. The Chinese property developers are some of the first to go. Many took on enormous debt to take advantage of the real estate boom. In the past month alone, prices for these bonds have fallen 22 cents on the dollar as default risks rise.[57]

In the past, Chinese state banks would sometimes step in and buy foreign bonds. For example, Greentown China Holdings Ltd. avoided a default in 2009 by paying off $400 million of its foreign bonds. They raised money through lightly regulated Chinese trust companies. This exit strategy is probably closed. China's banking regulator has been cracking down on trust companies' loans, specifically loans to Greentown.[58]

The foreign bond holders of Greentown were lucky to receive their investments back. Investors in Asia Aluminum were not so lucky. Asia's largest

---

[53] Tanya Powley, "Opportunities remain in emerging markets," *Financial Times*, www.ft.com, October 13 2011.

[54] David Oakley, "Emerging market dollar issues soar," *Financial Times*, www.ft.com, September 1, 2010.

[55] Henry Sanderson and Will McSheehy, "Bond Sales Beat Stocks in Busiest Start to a Year on Record: China Credit," *Bloomberg*, www.bloomberg.com/news/2011-01-23/bond-sales-beat-stocks-in-busiest-start-to-a-year-on-record-china-credit.html, January 24, 2011.

[56] Robert Cookson, "Chinese property boom starts to wobble," *Financial Times*, www.ft.com, September 29, 2011.

[57] Ibid.

[58] Laura Santini, "Greentown Buys Back Its Foreign Bonds: Property Firm Uses Loans to Pay Off Investors as China Relaxes Restrictions." *Wall Street Journal*, online.wsj.com/article/SB124155359838788625.html, May 6, 2009.

manufacturer of aluminum extruded products paid only 20 cents on the dollar for the senior bonds and only one cent on the dollar for the $800 million worth of junior bonds. An attempt by a Hong Kong bankruptcy court to liquidate the company's assets to get a better deal failed.

The problems are not just limited to China. Some Russian bond holders are beginning to worry. This year, the Russian ruble was the fourth best performer against the dollar. The combination of high yields and potential currency appreciation was irresistible. Many local Russian companies were happy to take advantage of this opportunity to issue international bonds denominated in rubles. It sounds like a good idea, unless problems develop. The market is illiquid, shallow, and new, so it will be more vulnerable to sell-offs than the dollar-denominated or local ruble bond markets.

The potential for trouble came in the recent example of the Bank of Moscow, a bank we discussed in Chapter 6. The Bank of Moscow is Russia's fifth largest bank, whose shareholders include Goldman Sachs and Credit Suisse. VTB, the state-controlled lender and Russia's second largest bank, recently bought 46.5% of the bank. What it found on the bank's books caused a scandal. There was a $14 billion hole in its balance sheet and questionable loans worth billions of dollars to businesses related to Bank of Moscow senior managers. This was bad enough. The real problem was that not only was the Bank of Moscow's $2 billion in foreign currency bonds placed in question, but so were $8 billion of VTB's own foreign currency bonds.

Many larger corporations in emerging markets are either state owned or have close ties to the government, which may not favor bond holders. Stiffing foreigners in pursuit of domestic policy goals is a time-honored practice.

Profiting from Emerging Markets

The emerging market story is certainly seductive. It is not just the investment banks of Wall Street that hear the siren's song. Famous academics do as well. A good example is Professor Burton Malkiel, author of the legendary *A Random Walk Down Wall Street*, first published in 1972 and now in its 10th edition. He is Professor Emeritus of Economics at Princeton University and a leading proponent of the efficient market hypothesis, which since its publication has shaped much of the thinking about investments.

In an essay published in the *Financial Times* in September 2011,[1] Professor Malkiel exhorted his readers to allocate far more of their assets to emerging markets. He believes that an examination of most portfolios would indicate that they are "severely underweighted to the most dynamic growth economies of the world." He has three excellent reasons for this hypothesis. The first is that the developed world has too much debt. Second, the developed world is too old. Third, the developed world has too few natural resources.

---

[1] Burton G. Malkiel, "Emerging stocks offer better returns and less risk," *Financial Times*, www.ft.com, September 19, 2011.

Why Malkiel Is Wrong

Of course, you cannot argue with two of these points. They are true. The developed world has too much debt. It is too old. But so what? Almost every country in Latin America has a smaller debt, at least for now. They all have young populations, and they all have natural resources. But, for most of the past 50 years, almost all of these economies have stagnated. To understand why, you have to look specifically at why Professor Malkiel's numbers are not telling him the truth.

His debt argument is this: according to the International Monetary Fund, the G20 advanced economies had a debt-to-gross domestic product ratio of more than 100 percent in 2010. By 2015, that percentage is projected to rise to 125 percent, while debt levels are less than one third of GDP in emerging markets and are projected to decline to only one-quarter by 2015. While this argument looks persuasive, we must remember that ten years ago the US budget was in surplus and its debt was declining so fast that there were worries about the availability of treasury bills. In contrast, we also should remember that it was only 13 years ago, during the Asian Currency Crisis, that many of the Asian tigers had to be bailed out by the IMF.

The reason why the G20 has so much debt is that investors feel that they will be paid back. Many of the G20 countries could easily do so by slightly raising taxes or lessening entitlements. Many emerging markets—specifically China—can't really collect taxes and have billions in hidden debt.

It is true that Greece may default on its loans, but it has been in default for about 50% of the time since its recognition as an independent country in 1832. Greece was bailed out in 1987 and was threatened with expulsion from the EU in 1991.[2] Defaults and restructurings have occurred in much of Latin America, Russia, and even China.

Professor Malkiel's age argument is that the dependency ratio, the ratio of retirees to young people in a country's population, is rising sharply in the developed world, while the emerging markets remain young. In theory, a younger population means faster growth. But, this first assumes that retirement age remains static and that the young can actually be productively employed. As we have seen, the world is filled with poorly educated young people who have few prospects for employment. If the countries that this population inhabits are not good at creating jobs, they could become politically unstable,

---

[2] Tony Barber, "Greece pays price of scrutiny for help," *Financial Times*, www.ft.com February 12, 2010.

ensuring that growth is cut short. This is already occurring more often than steady growth.

Finally, Professor Malkiel argues that hydrocarbons, metals, land, and water are finite and, in the end, the (inflation-adjusted) prices of commodities will rise. So, there are "excellent long-term investment opportunities in companies and countries with abundant natural resources—not only oil and metals, but also arable land and abundant water."[3]

Here, Professor Malkiel is at least partly wrong. Many emerging markets like India and China have limited natural resources, especially perhaps the most important ones like land and water. In contrast, new technologies like fracking have allowed the discoveries of vast new sources of hydrocarbons in developed countries. As the price rises, countries with well-developed markets have shown themselves exceptionally able to substitute commodities, including energy.

So, the esteemed professor makes the grievous but common error of assuming that present statistical trajectories will continue indefinitely into the future. He assumes that China will always grow and that Saudi Arabia's vast oil reserves will always have value. He also assumes that the economic inputs of labor, capital, and commodities are the only ingredients of economic growth. In fact, these inputs are useless unless the government provides the legal infrastructure to encourage enterprise. Egypt's large young population may be more of a problem than a benefit unless it makes major reforms to protect smaller enterprises.

Yet, if one of the leading lights of economics is seduced by simple misconceptions, others are as well. For example, I just received an advertisement for a conference on Brazil. The e-mail proudly states that this conference is the best way to make money, because "If you want long-term, profitable investments, it's no secret Brazil is all the buzz."[4] Advertisements are routinely run on television financial channels like CNBC promoting the brokerage's expertise in emerging markets. What is especially interesting about both Professor Malkiel's essay and the e-mail is that they were published in late September 2011 when the MSCI Emerging Index had fallen 30 percent in five months.

---

[3] Burton G. Malkiel, "Emerging stocks offer better returns and less risk," *Financial Times*, www.ft.com, September 19, 2011.

[4] Brazil Investment Summit USA 2011, e-mail message to the author, September 26, 2011.

Why Don't They Invest in Themselves?

Most investors in developed countries ignore one of the best indicators of the investment climate of emerging markets: emerging market investors. Investors in emerging markets know their countries far better than we do. Like purchases or sales by corporate principals of their own company's stock, their actions are an important indicator of the potential for their country's growth.

Indian corporate investments outside of the country through joint ventures and wholly owned subsidiaries almost doubled to $5.5 billion in the second quarter of 2011. "Despite sitting on ample cash, Indian companies have been reluctant to invest locally because of uncertain economic environment, lack of policy impetus, high inflation and the rising interest rates."[5] Brazilian investors prefer bonds and hold substantial liquid assets. Equity funds make up only a tenth of the market. Wealthy individuals continue to hold liquid assets outside the country in offshore centers such as Miami, New York, or Switzerland.[6] The average price for high-end London real estate in September of 2011 is 4.5% higher than the last price peak reached in March 2008 due to purchases by wealthy Russians. This is in turn due to a degree of uncertainty connected with the Russian elections.[7] Their investments in London pale compared to the massive holdings in Cypriot banks.

But, the biggest anomaly is China. China is the fastest-growing economy in the world, but its government is long on US dollars. It owns more than a trillion and a half to say nothing of its holdings of Japanese yen and Euros. Its state-owned companies are making purchases of foreign corporations whenever possible, and even its corrupt officials have shipped $124 billion abroad.[8] The glaring question is, if things are so great in China, why not invest it there?

---

[5] "India Inc Reluctant to Invest Locally, Doubles Overseas Investment," *Economic Times*, http://economictimes.indiatimes.com/news/news-by-company/corporate-trends/india-inc-reluctant-to-invest-locally-doubles-overseas-investment/articleshow/9891192.cms?ftcamp=crm/email/201197/nbe/beyondbricsNewYork/product, September 7, 2011.

[6] "Brazil: Financial services report," *Economist Intelligence Unit*, www.eiu.com/index.asp?layout=ib3Article&article_id=1398329324&pubtypeid=1132462498&country_id=1480000148&category_id=775133077, July 5, 2011.

[7] "Uncertainty at Home Fueling Russian Purchases in London," *Moscow Times*, www.themoscowtimes.com/business/article/uncertainty-at-home-fueling-russian-purchases-in-london/444728.html, October 4, 2011.

[8] Jamil Anderlini, "Corrupt officials took $124bn out of China," *Financial Times*, www.ft.com, June 16, 2011.

This does not mean that you cannot make money in emerging markets. You can. Investors have made large profits in emerging markets—but only if they recognize the rules.

How to Invest

The idea that emerging markets are somehow decoupled from developed markets has always been simply wrong. Emerging markets do not continue to grow when the developed markets are in recession. Emerging markets have almost always been a "high beta" play on the US and Europe. In other words, they outperform the US and European averages when they do well and underperform when the developed world goes into recession. Given the volatility of emerging markets, this is what one would expect.

Besides degree, the differences have to with timing. Many emerging markets hit their pre-2008 crash highs in the fall of 2007 and started to decline. Some have never really stopped. Others hit their bottoms in the fall of 2008 rather than six months later.

One reason for the slight variation has to do with the size of these markets. Many are small relative to the much larger economies of the US and China. Many Asian markets started to slide when the Chinese market went into to decline on October 31, 2007 and started to rise when China started to pour stimulus money into its economy.

Pay Attention to Cycles

So, like investing in a developed market, investing in an emerging market requires the investor to determine the phase of the cycle. Also, making comparisons may not be especially helpful. For example, according to the *Financial Times* in early October 2011, "emerging markets look oversold. They now sell for a lower multiple of book value than the World index, despite superior growth prospects."[9] Emerging markets generally sell for a lower multiple of the world index, because along with the superior growth prospects, there are also much larger risk issues.

Depending on the country, investors have to be aware that there may not be any cycle. There are markets like Saudi Arabia and Vietnam that have recovered but never even came close to their all-time highs, reached in 2005 and

---

[9] Lex, "Emerging Markets: Decoupling Decoupled," *Financial Times*, www.ft.com, October 4, 2011.

2007, respectively. Even though they made substantial recoveries after 2008, China and Hong Kong never reached the heights they attained in 2007. China's recent highs are only 50 percent of the 2007 peak. In contrast, the S&P in its recent rally reached within 12 percent of its pre-crash high.

There are also examples of high-growth countries like Brazil and Japan that after a spurt of rapid growth languish for 20 years. There is a high probability that China may fall into this category, with implications for countries in Asia that have enjoyed derivative growth from China. There are also countries like Thailand and Malaysia whose growth rates over the past ten years barely exceed two percent. In fact, there is a lot of evidence to suggest that the recent growth in emerging markets is in fact an anomaly, not a blue print for the future. The past 50 years are littered with countries that were supposed to mature into the developed category, but instead merely stagnated.

Go with the Momentum

One major influence on these markets (and all markets) is simply momentum. Emerging markets tend to do well at certain times because investors believe that they will do well. Riding a wave of momentum can be very profitable, provided an investor does not always believe in the justifications provided for the move. The crash of a momentum-driven trend can also be highly profitable, although at this time it is difficult to short some of the country-specific ETFs. Since many of these markets are highly concentrated, it may be possible to short other proxies.

It's All About the Country

A discerning eye to the specific country is also exceptionally important. In the fall of 2011, it appears that with the decline of China, much of Asia will not have the stellar returns that have been expected. Many of these markets have also reached all-time highs, which is a bad sign for future investments, although a good time to short a particular market. Investing in any bubble is a very bad way to try to make money. Looking for the reversion to mean is a far safer strategy.

Since the information coming out of China tends to be severely distorted, it will be difficult to accurately assess the state of its economy. This difficulty extends even to the Chinese, who have created a system that rewards disinformation and tends to punish truth. The distortions of information and the needs of the party will make it ever more difficult for the government to make some of the changes that Western economists are fond of suggesting and the Chinese are tired of hearing.

With the problems mounting, the Chinese economy and the emerging market economies of Asia will most likely have issues until at least 2013. It will be difficult for the Chinese to reinflate because of persistent inflation and a mountain of bad loans left over from the 2009 to 2010 spree. Government economic policies have their own momentum, which only changes when the government does, and the Chinese government shows no sign of changing.

Although the stimulus of China may be gone, stimulus from reform is always available. Better government policies could potentially lead to better corporate governance, more transparency, better information, efficient allocation of capital, a more-educated work force, protection of civil and property rights, and infrastructure investments. Powerful forces able to exert power simply because they can are arrayed against these reforms. There are no legal limits to their reach, and so they can take whatever they want. Countries that have these limits have the best chance of achieving the real growth assumed to be a part of every emerging market. But, it is often easier and faster to build a concrete physical infrastructure of roads, ports, damns, and electric grids than to change a legal infrastructure. Corrupt vested interests can skim government infrastructure projects, but certainly don't take kindly to losing their privileges.

The countries with the best chance of achieving this growth are the democratic ones, because they can at least harness the collective intelligence of their citizens to achieve the best policies. At this time, the most hopeful would be Brazil, India, Indonesia, Chile, Turkey, South Africa, and many of the countries of Eastern Europe, especially Poland. The most likely candidate to be the new engine out of a possible recession is the country that always leads, the US, but perhaps not any time soon. If the US does let its economy achieve what it can, it will no doubt take Mexico with it.

The countries with diminished growth prospects are those whose governments and policies cannot change. These include countries like China, Russia, and Vietnam. They also include their single-party state relatives, authoritarian régimes of all stripes, and the plethora of unstable and failed states.

Emerging Markets Are Tied to Established Markets

The point about emerging markets is that part of their growth story has to do with global growth. There is no decoupling, and we are all in this together as never before. Furthermore, we have been here before.

I have observed that you can chart economic growth from the history of architectural styles. No one builds large buildings during recessions. You need economic growth and credit generated by trade to create great architecture. When you do, the men and women who commission these buildings want nothing but the latest look.

As you travel the world, whether in Bucharest or Buenos Aires, you will see reflections of the late 19th century Beaux Arts style. It reached from the furthest corner of the world in the Teatro Amazonas in Manaus, Brazil to the gaudy mansions of where I live in Newport, Rhode Island, in the United States. This economic boom brought many of the riches of the emerging markets of the day to the developed markets of Europe. It made Europe and emerging markets like the United States and Brazil rich. All that ended with the end of the uniform global laws imposed by the colonial empires. The 30 years of war at the beginning of the 20th century and the 45 years of cold war that followed did the rest to kill one of the most productive economic periods in history and the first true era of globalization. Instead of achieving economic growth and perhaps political maturity, the world stagnated until the late 20th century. Despite many technological advances, globalization was stopped in its tracks as the world was divided between capitalism and communism and many of today's most dynamic countries were caught in the middle of proxy wars.

Before the First World War, writers believed that war was impossible because of the economic interrelationships between the European powers, but war happened anyway. Many writers now believe that the forces of globalization will help many emerging markets achieve the growth that should have been theirs many years ago. It certainly is possible. The potential for hope is there. As always, dazzling new technologies seem to offer methods to leapfrog ahead. But, the institutions that are required for a great leap forward cannot be constructed overnight, and their construction will be as uneven and varied as the countries themselves. To make a profit, even a potentially very large profit, from investing in these countries, it is essential to keep an eye on the progress.

Sources of Information on Emerging Markets

Investing anywhere requires an obsessive observance of a constantly changing situation. Minimizing risks and taking advantage of opportunities is an unrelenting battle. I do not believe in any strategy that assumes things will remain the same, nor do I believe in any strategy that involves constant trading. Information is constantly changing, but much of the information is either withheld or misunderstood. Revelations and insight sometimes happen after the events themselves, and it may take time for markets to adjust. So a continuous reevaluation of the information is an absolute necessity.

Newspapers and Magazines

The gold standard for information is the *Financial Times*[1] and *The Economist*.[2] Both publications combine excellent reporting and discerning analysis. From

---

[1] www.ft.com/home/us

[2] www.economist.com/

my perspective, it would be impossible to invest internationally without digesting a large amount of what they both have to offer.

There are a few other information providers that are very good. *Bloomberg,*[3] *Reuters,*[4] *BBC,*[5] and *Agence France-Presse (AFP)*[6] are often excellent sources of information. I usually use digests to get a general overview of the dynamic situations of international markets and sort through the articles to find those that are of use.

I do use stories from the *Wall Street Journal.*[7] Many are often excellent. However, I find the *Wall Street Journal's* perspective a bit parochial. It is centered on information that is either about to or will have impact on US markets. In that area, it is excellent and second to none. However, when its journalists, and especially its analysts or commentators, wander further afield, the limits of their bias get in the way.

For up-to-date information, I usually use *MarketWatch,*[8] where I do interviews. I also prefer the graphs on *Bloomberg* and *Yahoo Finance.*[9]

Before Google was able to instantly translate languages, the only source of information for emerging markets was local English language papers, and even with Google's priceless gift they are often still the best source. Most of their readers are part of an international community. They are used to and demand unbiased and accurate information. They are quick to spot slanted reporting. These papers have traditions of excellence to uphold. My guess is that local authorities often leave them alone and don't try too hard to influence their reporting. Governments are usually less concerned about papers that report to a small group of foreigners than information available in their citizens' native languages.

One of the best is the venerable *South China Morning Post.*[10] Published in Hong Kong, it gives an excellent perspective on China. So much so that the

---

[3] www.bloomberg.com/

[4] www.reuters.com/

[5] www.bbc.co.uk/

[6] www.afp.com/afpcom/en/

[7] http://online.wsj.com/home-page

[8] www.marketwatch.com/

[9] http://finance.yahoo.com/

[10] www.scmp.com/portal/site/SCMP/

Chinese authorities have occasionally felt the need to punish the *Post* or its reporters for their honest reporting.

Also published in China, *Caixin,*[11] of Caixin Media Company Ltd., is not exactly an English-language newspaper, but it is published in English. Caixin Media is a Chinese company that publishes two Chinese papers. For English speakers, it also publishes *Caixin* online. *Caixin* was originally founded by Hu Shuli, the former founding editor of *Caijing Magazine*. *Caijing* was known for its investigative reporting, but in 2009 Hu Shuli and the majority of reporters became concerned with its independence and left en mass to create *Caixin*. In its new form, it has continued to be a source of important unbiased information about China, but there are definite limits to what it can report.

On the other end of the spectrum is *The People's Daily.*[12] *The People's Daily* is the official newspaper of the Central Committee of the Communist Party of China and published through its news and information company, Xinhua. Since 1998, *The People's Daily* has published an English-language online site. What is published in English often bears little relationship to what is published in Chinese. It is interesting to read not only what is published but also what is not published.

In contrast to China is India, where free speech is protected and English is spoken by an estimated 176 million people. India has a plethora of excellent newspapers. Both the *Financial Express*[13] and the *Economic Times*[14] are very good. My columns are published in the excellent and feisty *MoneyLife.*[15] I also have published articles in *The Analyst,*[16] a magazine for certified financial analysts in India.

My columns are also published in another dual-language financial newspaper in the UAE. *Alrroya*[17] is the first regional financial newspaper. It is published by Imedia. Imedia LLC was established in August 2008, and it is the UAE's first fully integrated media company.

---

[11] http://english.caixin.cn/

[12] http://english.peopledaily.com.cn/

[13] www.financialexpress.com/

[14] http://economictimes.indiatimes.com/

[15] www.moneylife.in/

[16] www.iupindia.in/analyst.asp

[17] http://english.alrroya.com/

For Russia, I read *The Moscow Times*.[18] The best was the English language version of *Kommersant*, but that was shut down in 2008. Although a general newspaper, *The Moscow Times* often has excellent articles about various aspects of business in Russia.

Other excellent local English language newspapers include *The Taipei Times*[19] in Taiwan, *The Korea Times*[20] in South Korea, and *The Nation*[21] in Thailand.

Experts

Professor Philip Tetlock, whom we met in Chapter 1, has written extensively on why pundits and experts are often wrong and how their opinions are no more accurate than those of ordinary people. David H. Freedman's book *Wrong*[22] also made this point, especially about models. These issues are especially problematic for financial commentators and economists.

After years of researching, I often see the same statistic showing up in many different places. Experts, among their other failings, have a tendency to follow herd. When I finally confirmed this tendency, I started making a reasonably decent living by finding out what the experts recommended and doing the opposite.

However, this is not true of all experts. There are a few that I follow who have not only the ability to think differently, but also the ability to be right.

One of the best economists is Michael Pettis. Pettis is a professor at Peking University's Guanghua School of Management, where he specializes in Chinese financial markets. He generally posts rather long articles on *Seeking Alpha*.[23] He also writes articles for an assortment of financial newspapers including *The Wall Street Journal* and *The Financial Times*.

I know that Chinese economist Andy Xie is good because he has been fired for it. He was once Morgan Stanley's star Asia-Pacific economist, but was fired because an email of his was leaked. In the email, he criticized Lee Hsien

---

[18] www.themoscowtimes.com/index.php

[19] www.taipeitimes.com/

[20] www.koreatimes.co.kr/www/index.asp

[21] www.nationmultimedia.com/

[22] David H. Freedman. *Wrong: Why Experts Keep Failing Us—and How to Know When Not to Trust Them* (Boston: Little Brown and Company, 2010).

[23] http://seekingalpha.com/author/michael-pettis

Loong, Singapore's prime minister, and he scorned Singapore's claim to have overseen an economic miracle. He also derided the Association of South East Asian Nations as a "failure" for its inability to lift economic growth over the past decade. Such honesty was unbecoming to Morgan Stanley's reputation, so they dumped him. He writes weekly columns for *Caixin*[24] and advises clients.

The best columnist for the *Financial Times* is the present editor of the "Lex" column, John Authers.[25] Mr. Authers used to write "The Short View," which is now ably written by James Mackintosh.[26] Besides "Lex," Mr. Authers writes the "Long View" column.

James Kynge is the editor of *China Confidential,*[27] a research service of the *Financial Times*. Formerly, he was their China Bureau Chief. Any article of his is well worth reading.

General Resources

The *Doing Business Project,*[28] which was first launched in 2002, looks at domestic small- and medium-sized companies and measures the regulations applied to them throughout their life cycle. The report is created as part of a joint project of the World Bank and International Finance Corporation. While far from perfect, it does give a rough guide to the economic efficiency of a legal infrastructure, which in my view is the only true measure of the potential for sustainable economic growth.

Transparency International's *Corruption Perceptions Index (CPI)*[29] is another exceptionally important method of judging a country's long term competitive outlook. When corruption is high, it means that the system is distorted to help specific local power groups, not foreign investors.

Wikipedia[30] is one of the great blessings of the Internet. Studies have shown that it is just as accurate as respected reference sources.

---

[24] http://english.caixin.cn/

[25] www.ft.com/intl/comment/columnists/johnauthers

[26] www.ft.com/intl/markets/short-view

[27] www.ft.com/intl/comment/columnists/james-kynge

[28] www.doingbusiness.org/

[29] www.transparency.org/policy_research/surveys_indices/cpi

[30] www.wikipedia.org/

CIA Fact Book[31] is also a great source for facts, figures, and statistics about the world.

Books

Japan's policy trap: dollars, deflation, and the crisis of Japanese finance (Washington, DC: The Brookings Institution Press, 2002), by Akio Mikuni and R. Taggart Murphy is not only one of the best books on Japan's economy, but also one of the best books on how different an Asian government's relationship to an economy can be. It stands as a stark reminder of what can happen to an investment and export growth model. Often there have been stories comparing the US to Japan. I believe a more accurate comparison would be China and Japan.

Joe Studwell's books *China Dream* (London: Profile Business, 2005) and *Asian Godfathers* (New York: Grove Press, 2008) both provide excellent and accurate studies of how business is actually done in Asia. Although he writes about Asia, the structures are the same in many emerging markets.

A professor at MIT's Sloan business school, Yasheng Huang, has written two incredibly well-researched studies of China, *Capitalism with Chinese Characteristics* (New York: Cambridge University Press, 2008) and *Selling China: Foreign Direct Investment During the Reform Era* (New York: Cambridge University Press, 2005). Both are devastating studies about the myth of state-led capitalism.

I really couldn't read much of Professor Avinash K. Dixit's *Lawlessness and Economics: Alternative Modes of Governance* (Princeton, New Jersey: Princeton University Press, 2004). I am not fluent in his language of mathematics. However, when he does get around to writing in English, his points are direct and clear. He is the origin of the concept of a rule-based system versus a relationship-based system. Just the words "relationship-based system" are an enormous improvement over the term used by sociologists, which is "second- and third-party social norms."

Good Capitalism, Bad Capitalism, and the Economics of Growth and Prosperity by William J. Baumol, Robert E. Litan, and Carl J. Schramm (New Haven, Connecticut: Yale University Press, 2009) is an excellent portrait of the various types of capitalism and a warning that we should be careful about how we talk about markets.

---

[31] https://www.cia.gov/library/publications/the-world-factbook/

Jasper Becker was a superb reporter for the *South China Morning Post* until he published the truth too often and the authorities in Beijing put pressure on the paper to get rid of him. He has a string of excellent books on China, specifically *The Chinese* (Oxford: Oxford University Press, 2002).

Game Theory and the Law (Cambridge, Massachusetts: Harvard University Press, 1994) by Douglas Baird, Robert Gertner, and Randal Picker was a revelation for me. Like most Americans, and especially like American lawyers, I had specific views about the utility of law, its function for governance, its utility within society, and its impact on markets. I was wrong.

The impact of Richard A. Posner's *Economic Analysis of the Law* (New York: Aspen Press, 2007) is hard to underestimate. Besides creating a whole new area of study for law, it has slowly begun to have some influence on the thinking of economists, where it is desperately needed.

I am also exceptionally proud of my own books. *Investing in China* (Westport, Connecticut: Quorum Books, 2002) was published almost ten years ago, but there are few if any predictions that are not totally accurate. To update it, you could just substitute different anecdotes. The predictions in *Freedom: America's Competitive Advantage in the Global Market* (Westport, Connecticut: Praeger Publishers, 2007) are also totally accurate, especially the ones about different labor markets.

If I have ever written anything that has value, it is because of the great economist Mancur Olson. Reading his books was a revelation. Interestingly enough, if you ask a room full of financial professionals if they have ever heard of him, you draw a blank. On the other hand, if you ask them if they have heard of "free riders" and "collective-action problems," they all raise their hands. Olson wrote about the issue in *The Logic of Collective Action: Public Goods and the Theory of Groups* (Cambridge, Massachusetts: Harvard University Press, 1971). Later he extended the idea in *The Rise and Decline of Nations: Economic Growth, Stagflation, and Social Rigidities* (New Haven, Connecticut: Yale University Press, 1984). Finally, before his premature death, he wrote *Power and Prosperity: Outgrowing Communist and Capitalist Dictatorships*, which was published posthumously (New York: Basic Books, 2000).

Index

CPSIA information can be obtained at www.ICGtesting.com
Printed in the USA
LVOW061212261211

261069LV00004B/60/P